Elaine May |

Contemporary Film Directors

Edited by Justus Nieland and Jennifer Fay

The Contemporary Film Directors series provides concise, well-written introductions to directors from around the world and from every level of the film industry. Its chief aims are to broaden our awareness of important artists, to give serious critical attention to their work, and to illustrate the variety and vitality of contemporary cinema. Contributors to the series include an array of internationally respected critics and academics. Each volume contains an incisive critical commentary, an informative interview with the director, and a detailed filmography.

For a list of books in the series, please see our website at www.press.uillinois.edu.

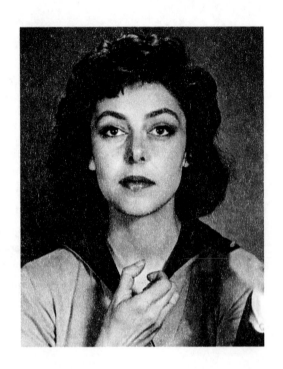

Elaine May |

Elizabeth Alsop

UNIVERSITY OF
ILLINOIS PRESS
Urbana, Chicago, and Springfield

Frontispiece: *Morning Call* newspaper, 1959, via Wikimedia Commons (https://en.wikipedia.org/wiki/File:Elaine_May_-_publicity1.jpg#filelinks)

Library of Congress Cataloging-in-Publication Data

Names: Alsop, Elizabeth, author.
Title: Elaine May / Elizabeth Alsop.
Description: Urbana : University of Illinois Press, 2025. | Series: Contemporary film directors | Includes bibliographical references and index.
Identifiers: LCCN 2024025232 (print) | LCCN 2024025233 (ebook) | ISBN 9780252046490 (cloth) | ISBN 9780252088582 (paperback) | ISBN 9780252047800 (ebook)
Subjects: LCSH: May, Elaine, 1932—Criticism and interpretation. | Motion picture producers and directors—United States. | Women motion picture producers and directors—United States. | Women screenwriters—United States. | Women comedians—United States.
Classification: LCC PN1998.3.M3955 A47 2025 (print) | LCC PN1998.3.M3955 (ebook) | DDC 791.4302/33092—dc23/eng/20240821
LC record available at https://lccn.loc.gov/2024025232
LC ebook record available at https://lccn.loc.gov/2024025233

To my daughter, Lucinda

Contents |

This book was a project of the pandemic. During the initial lockdown I decided to watch all of Elaine May's films in chronological order. When I got to *Ishtar*, I was flabbergasted: *This* was the movie everyone had maligned? The first sequence alone was easily one of the funniest things I had ever seen. I feel lucky that I've had the chance to write about films I love this much and to take on a project that brought me a lot of joy during some difficult times.

When it comes to acknowledgments, I need to start by thanking my union, the PSC-CUNY, which provided me as a pretenure faculty member with the time I needed to complete this manuscript. Additional PSC-CUNY research awards supported writing during the summer. My thanks also go to the National Endowment for the Humanities: a 2022 Summer Stipend offered crucial financial support and ensured my timely completion of the manuscript.

CUNY's Faculty Fellowship Publication Program offered me not only time but also invaluable feedback from a community of peers. I want to thank Ava Chin, as well as my fellow FFPP members and CUNY colleagues, Lissette Acosta, Jade Charon, Eve Eure, Shon McCarthy, and Mudiwa Pettus, for engaging so constructively with the drafts I shared.

I am fortunate to have colleagues who offered consistent encouragement and guidance throughout the many stages of academic book writing. Laurel Harris and Tahneer Oksman provided incisive input on my book proposal, as did Sean O'Sullivan, who was an early and enthusiastic supporter of this project. Joseph McElhaney allowed me to review his then-unpublished essay on May and, with Sean, provided a letter of recommendation for my successful application for the NEH Summer Stipend. I am grateful to them both.

Books in this series usually conclude with an original interview with the director. I assumed that speaking with May would be impossible—as it turned out, I was right—but I deeply appreciate those who helped me try. Steve Macfarlane took the time to connect me with Miriam Bale, who was kind enough to introduce me to Julian Schlossberg, May's friend and collaborator. His efforts to obtain answers for the written questions I shared were no less than heroic. Much like *Seinfeld*'s Elaine Benes, recapping her attempts to "beat the Van Wyck," I'd like to think that when it comes to getting an interview, "I came as close as anyone ever has," at least in recent years.

The notable exception, of course, would be Haden Guest, who sat down with Elaine May for two incredible conversations at the Harvard Film Archive in 2010. I am immensely grateful to Haden for allowing me to reprint one of those discussions here.

I also need to thank the many colleagues, in and out of film studies, who provided informal support and whose interest in and inquiries about the project offered a welcome boost: Maria San Filippo, Martha Shearer, Maya Montañez Smukler, Jason Mittell, Kevin Ferguson, Paula Massood, Hillary Miller, Yael Levy, David Gerstner, Edward Miller, Amy Herzog, Susan Kerns, Nancy K. Miller, Alix Beeston, Gabriel Hankins, James Richardson, Sarah Zeller-Berkman, Mariette Bates, Carla Marquez-Lewis, and Lauren Rosenblum. Giorgio Bertellini organized a panel at the SCMS annual conference in 2021, in which I was able to present an early excerpt from the book, and kindly shared his own resources on *Ishtar*'s reception. My thanks also go to Cindy Lucia and Bill Luhr, whose invitation to present at the Columbia Seminar in 2023 provided me with the chance to workshop a version of the *Ishtar* chapter.

I am indebted to two libraries. The New York Public Library's research division provided me with access to the Allen Room, an ideal space in which to write. Various librarians at the Library of Congress assisted me in accessing Neil Simon's original draft of *The Heartbreak Kid* among his papers.

I am fortunate that this book found a home with the Contemporary Film Directors series and with series editors as thoughtful and encouraging as Justus Nieland and Jennifer Fay. At the University of Illinois Press,

Danny Nasset provided early, instrumental support for this project and expert guidance throughout the process. Mariah Schaefer's meticulous instructions and continual assistance with a wide range of questions were invaluable. The two anonymous reviewers took exceptional care with my manuscript; I cannot thank them enough for their supremely attentive, intellectually generous, and insightful feedback. There's no doubt that their questions and suggestions improved the book. Mary M. Hill's careful copyedits likewise ensured the text's accuracy; any errors that remain are my own.

My network of friends and family sustained me during the writing process through their expressions of curiosity and confidence: Piyali Basak, Cody Campbell, Donna Rizzo, Somer Bingham, Nina Day Rauterkus, Stephanie Bencin, Tahneer Oksman, Kathryn Lanouette, Elyse Steinberg, I am lucky to have you. My parents, Reid and Annette, offered both emotional and more material support in the form of childcare; my sister, Cate, was always there to cheer me on, as were my aunt and uncle and my wonderful in-laws.

My deepest thanks go to my husband, Tony. When I was on the proverbial ledge, he channeled Warren Beatty's Lyle and talked me down. He has taken on more than his share of household labor to allow me time to research, write, and revise. My daughter Lucinda's interest in "my book" gave me the energy I needed to finish it. All of my love—and some cherry ripple kisses—to them both.

Elaine May |

An Unsentimental Education |

The Films of Elaine May

Elaine May's first film, *A New Leaf* (1971), opens in the midst of what appears to be a medical crisis. An EKG line pulses across a monitor while a middle-aged man looks on, grimacing. Across from him, two white-coated men work assiduously, one with stethoscope in hand, on an unseen body below. After some cross-cutting, the men relax: "She'll be alright now, Mr. Graham!" That reversal, however, immediately gives way to another as the camera tracks back and to the right, revealing that the patient in question is not a woman but a bright red sports car, in which the owner, Henry Graham, soon speeds off. The camera remains behind. "Usually needs a tune-up two to three times a week," one of the mechanics mutters, shaking his head. "I wonder what he does to her."

This opening scene not only provides a punch line at the very top of the film but also serves as a primer for May's cinema more generally. On the one hand, the scene features some of the themes—masculine insensibility, casual misogyny—that would regularly surface in the four films May directed between 1971 and 1987: *A New Leaf*, *The Heartbreak Kid* (1972), *Mikey and Nicky* (1976), and *Ishtar* (1987). But it also highlights May's scalpel-like methods, which frequently involve the strategic undercutting of narrative formulas, such that familiar scripts—the pained husband suffering at his beloved's bedside, for instance—are quickly and savagely flipped. In this way, May's filmmaking often converts tropes into vehicles of their own subversion, repurposing popular forms and phrases to reveal their cultural recalcitrance.

When *A New Leaf* was released in 1971, audiences would have already been familiar with May's acid sensibility, but in the context of improvisational theater, not film. It's an approach that animates the wildly successful comedy she performed with Mike Nichols in the late 1950s and early 1960s, a period in which Nichols and May became household names famed for improvisatory sketches that exposed the absurdities of postwar American life. Nichols and May were equally adept as social satirists and stage performers, and their routines extracted comedy from everyday scenarios—teenagers necking in a car, for instance, or two colleagues making water cooler chitchat.

Figure 1. Nichols and May perform a televised
public service announcement for Tax Day

A similarly sly, observational approach characterizes the numerous plays May wrote over the course of her career, which are at least as ruthless as her cinema in showcasing the inanities of US culture, with its sentimental attachment to ideals of upward mobility, domestic harmony, and material success. Considered cumulatively, May's body of work constitutes something like an unsentimental education, a darkly comic tour through the American middle-class psyche that manages to be at once richly pleasurable and absolutely unnerving. As May herself once put it, describing her ambitions in an early interview with the *New Yorker*, "The nice thing is to make an audience laugh and laugh and laugh, and shudder later" (Rice 75).

Yet even as May's films share with her theatrical work certain thematic concerns along with a sardonic wit and a foundation in Jewish comedy, they also make new and newly discomfiting demands of the audience. Something *happens*, in other words, when May turns to the cinema and translates her career-long preoccupations into cinematic time and space, putting the dialogue-based humor of her stage comedy into contact with the representational regimes and rhetorical possibilities of narrative film. Much like *A New Leaf*'s opening scene, her films often proceed through misdirection, mobilizing the generic conventions of commercial filmmaking while introducing ideas and affects these forms had historically suppressed. In *A New Leaf*, for example, it is the aggression inherent in Hollywood courtship narratives that May brings to the surface, turning subtext, under the guise of lighthearted comedy, into text.

The form of May's cinema, meanwhile, reflects the influence of her background in improvisational performance. The results, evident in her films' exploratory rhythms, use of long and often static takes, and detachment from a single character's point of view, are frequently at odds with the narrative temporalities and aesthetic practices of commercial cinema, even of the supposedly loosened New Hollywood variety. May's willingness to prioritize performance and comic discovery over cinematic decorum results in a relentless, even perverse realism, one that privileges the excavation of behavioral truths over narrative efficiency, generic consistency, or ideological convenience.

This book explores May's unique brand of cinematic nonconformism as it manifests across the four films she directed in the 1970s and 1980s, a period of time in which, significantly, she was one of the only women (and often the *only* woman) directing studio features in Hollywood.[1] The book pays particular attention to the way May worked within popular Hollywood genres and succeeded in infusing them with her own comic sensibility. Most distinctive may be the vision of masculinity that emerges collectively from her four films and that differs noticeably from the one on view in much American filmmaking of the 1970s, an era in which chauvinism's fallout for women was often presented more as bleak fact than cause for outrage. As feminist critic Molly Haskell has suggested, when it came to New Hollywood, "the sexual revolution turned out to be more about fucking than feminism" ("Mad Housewives" 19). Inevitably, the book also attends to May's progressive marginalization within the film industry and the outsized difficulties she encountered in the process of realizing—or attempting to realize—her uncompromising vision.

A central aim of this book, then, is not only to redress May's omission from the historical record but also to reposition her as a major American director, one who has to date remained "hiding in plain sight" (Rosenbaum). In the process, it also rebuts the narratives of failure that have dogged May since the studio-engineered disaster that was *Ishtar* and her subsequent dispatch to "director jail." Even before *Ishtar*'s release, coverage of May had been distorted by journalists' disproportionate focus on her persona rather than her creative output. In a rare 2010 conversation at the Harvard Film Archives, May alluded to the media's obsession with policing personal behavior, "the fact of who you were married to, and that you had been drinking, you know, all through the summer" (see the next section, "An Interview with Elaine May"). Meanwhile, May's own silence—she effectively stopped granting interviews in 1975—has allowed speculation to circulate unchecked.

To offset both the misinformation and the predisposition toward the personal that have characterized discussions of her career, I begin this study by situating May's films within their broader cultural and historical contexts, including the rise of New Hollywood and the emergence of feminist film criticism in the 1970s. Only then do I pivot to biography, noting the ways in which secondary accounts have often served to perpetuate myths about May's life and career, before surveying the richly suggestive evidence furnished by May's own extensive body of work for stage and screen. In this way, I hope to lay a foundation for the fullest possible understanding of May's four feature films: to consider them both in conversation and in tension with trends in classical and postclassical Hollywood cinema, as well as in relation to May's achievements as a comedian, playwright, screenwriter, and performer over the course of her decades-long career. Such an approach has as its goal both the elucidation of May's films and some more measured assessment of the way in which her movies, over the course of protracted and often highly contentious shoots, may at times have fallen short of her goals.

May in New (and Old) Hollywood

A survey of the films May directed reveals the shifting nature of her comic targets: from the deeply unromantic comedies, *A New Leaf* and *The Heartbreak Kid*, which present heterosexual coupledom as an unqualified catastrophe; to *Mikey and Nicky*, a deconstructed gangster film that exposes the brutality at the heart of the American bromance; to *Ishtar*, May's riff on Bob Hope and Bing Crosby's *Road to Morocco* (1942), which provides a farcical take on both US and Hollywood politics and the tolerance for dysfunctional white masculinity that defines both. In each of these films, May's wry detachment from her male protagonists generates both comic enjoyment and intense discomfort, as viewers are forced to register the inconvenient truths that these characters, who range from the clueless to the sociopathic, are unable to.

The result is a group of films that don't fit comfortably in a single cinematic tradition or time period. On the one hand, May's unorthodoxy seems in line with the priorities of New Hollywood, an era in which iconoclasm, at least in certain forms, became a sought-after and highly mythologized commodity. That all four of May's films are about the "idiocy of men," for instance, would appear to make them exemplary of the American New Wave's fabled investment in antiheroism and downbeat plots (Hoberman, "In *Mikey and Nicky*"). In other ways, however, May was functionally at odds with the era's gestalt. The haplessness of May's men, for instance, differentiates them from the decade's superficially antiheroic—but residually romantic—male protagonists. And unlike many of her 1970s peers, and with the exception of *Mikey and Nicky*, May worked squarely in the realm of comedy and in the tradition of Jewish comedy specifically; she populated her films with schmucks who were united by a seemingly boundless capacity for cluelessness and self-deceit. Together, these characters—May's "gallery of the oblivious," as Richard Brody has called them—arguably constitute as robust a challenge to the status quo as the more self-consciously countercultural archetypes, the Easy Riders and Raging Bulls, that would come to define New Hollywood in the popular imagination (see Brody, "To Wish").[2]

May's distance from her better-known male contemporaries might best be measured by her fundamentally opportunistic approach to genre. In contrast to the emerging generation of film-school-trained directors who engaged in what Todd Berliner has termed "genre bending" or "genre breaking" (90–99), May's lighter, less reverent approach indicates a director comparatively unburdened by cinephilia, more inclined toward social criticism than self-reflexivity. Indeed, it's worth recalling that unlike the era's so-called movie brats—Martin Scorsese, Paul Schrader, Francis Ford Coppola, George Lucas, William Friedkin—May was self-taught, a convert to filmmaking rather than a true believer, a writer who turned director only when Paramount pressured her into accepting the role on *A New Leaf*.[3]

Working with or through genre also permitted May to operate at a communicative remove, to adopt what Brad Stevens and Joe McElhaney have variously described as a "reticent" or "dispassionate" style that strategically leaves viewers to render their own judgments (Stevens, "Male Narrative" 77). While the era in which May was active as a director may be best known for films that embraced the opportunity to feature explicit sexuality and violence or to experiment with forms of stylization gleaned from European art cinema—from *Bonnie and Clyde* (1967), *The Graduate* (1967), and *Carnal Knowledge* (1971) to *The Wild Bunch* (1969), *Taxi Driver* (1974), and *Chinatown* (1974)—May's films engage in more subtle acts of subversion, paired with moments of slapstick and unexpected sweetness. As Haden Guest observes in "The Comic Vision of Elaine May," May's films "strike an unusual balance between the abrasive and the affectionate," their critiques of self-deluding men offset by a loopy, somewhat distracted sensibility. As a result—and with the exception of the more emphatically uncommercial *Mikey and Nicky*—the more radical dimensions of her filmmaking tend to become evident in the aggregate and on repeat viewings rather than leaping forth from a single scene or shot. Watching May's films, one gets the sense that she was working under the cover of genre and made a habit of "throwing away" rather than underscoring some of her screenplay's most barbed lines. In *Ishtar*, for instance, we could easily miss the droll humor of Isabelle Adjani, a leftist militant, begging the dopey American, played by Dustin Hoffman, to "keep [her] secret without trying to understand it."

While May's 1970s films might share with others of the era a skeptical take on social mores, then, they differ significantly in their angle of approach. In a 1975 interview with Leonard Probst, May herself hinted at how susceptible even seemingly unfunny material could be to comic interpretation: "It's more a way of looking at things. You look at something one way and it's a disaster, you look at it another way and it's humorous. It depends on how you tilt your head" (135). Jackie Peters, a cousin of May's who also served as a production assistant on *Mikey and Nicky*, echoed this idea, recalling May's struggle to keep the humor out of what was inarguably her grimmest film: "[Elaine] complained about being unable to resist laugh lines and situations that occurred naturally to her comic imagination" (Canford 81).

With their wry tone and "tilted" gaze, May's films might seem to find a closer analogue in contemporaneous comedies such as *What's Up, Doc?* (1971), *Annie Hall* (1977), and *Modern Romance* (1981), which variously revised and revived screwball conventions for a new era. *A New Leaf* and *The Heartbreak Kid*, in particular, revisit the romantic antagonism and battle-of-the-sexes high jinks that characterize the cycle of classical Hollywood films that Stanley Cavell termed "comedies of remarriage." But if screwball comedies are ultimately, as Molly Haskell argues, "fables of love masquerading as hostility" (foreword 10), then May gives us something closer to the inverse: fables of hostility masquerading—just barely—as love.

By the same token, May's filmmaking might be understood in the context of the "Jewish New Wave," that "not-so-brief moment in the late 1960s and early '70s [when] a new wave of Jewish leading men and women . . . took Hollywood by storm" (Hoberman, "Hollywood's Jew Wave").[4] As Vincent Brooks notes in a recent reassessment, this "moment" was characterized not only by high-profile stars such as Barbra Streisand, Dustin Hoffman, and Elliott Gould but also by the emergence of a new generation of Jewish directors. Notably, May is the only woman included on the list Brooks has compiled, which fails to include other representative filmmakers such as Joan Micklin Silver and Claudia Weill. The omission is a reminder that it's possible both to acknowledge what May has in common with other Jewish comedians turned filmmakers such as Nichols, Allen, and Brooks and to observe the differentiating fact of her gender, which presented obstacles in 1970s and 1980s Hollywood with which her male peers did not have to contend.

In short, even as May collaborated with many of the figures most closely associated with this pivotal moment in American cinema—Nichols, Beatty, John Cassavetes—her films cannot easily be amalgamated into prevailing historical accounts of this period. Rather, her contributions to 1970s filmmaking, together with those of female contemporaries such as directors Weill, Silver, and Barbara Loden; editors Dede Allen and Marcia Lucas; production designers Polly Platt and Toby Carr Rafelson; and screenwriters Carole Eastman and Joan Tewkesbury, invite us to complicate the narrowly auteurist and still overwhelmingly macho narratives of New Hollywood that continue to circulate despite scholarly reassessments of the period.[5] Following the lead of scholars such as Maya Montañez Smukler, Martha Shearer, and Aaron Hunter, it is worth recognizing the extent to which the supposedly "liberated" moment in Hollywood actually wasn't and how substantially our history of "New" Hollywood needs finessing. If the existing discourse associates the period with muscular filmmaking, explicit sexuality and violence, and a newly visible "Method" of screen acting, it must also allow for innovations that look otherwise. Indeed, closer analyses of May's three films from the 1970s reveal that her work at once embodies the iconoclasm associated with the New Hollywood era while offering distinct and arguably more radical forms of critique.

Auteurism and Its Discontents

May's absence from histories of American filmmaking and the roster of American auteurs is the result less of unhappy accident than of deliberate exclusion. Later sections examine Columbia's campaign to tank *Ishtar*, whose infamously poor reception effectively consigned May to "director jail," and reveal the ways in which the film's status as a flop was predetermined by studio executives who, in May's words, "*so* killed it" (Guest, postscreening discussion about *Ishtar*). Unlike male collaborators such as Mike Nichols and Warren Beatty, who each experienced their own proportionally worse box-office bombs, May wouldn't be granted second or third chances. And like many female directors of her generation and subsequent ones, May didn't have the luxury of making mistakes, of having eccentricities, and of not turning profits while also, as Cassavetes has put it, "happen[ing] to be a woman" (qtd. in Canford 72). Indeed, May's career had barely started before she became a "cautionary tale about women directors" whose conflicts with Paramount during the making of *A New Leaf* and *Mikey and Nicky* appear to have set the stage for her eventual excommunication (Sheehan 8).

If May was a "studio victim," however, she was also a regular target of the press.[6] At least since *Mikey and Nicky*, journalists helped to establish the "construction of May as a director with an unruly filmmaking methodology," one whose cavalier disregard for money, time, and celluloid was destined to doom her directorial career (Heller-Nicholas 5). A case in point is David Blum's 1987 *New York* magazine cover story on *Ishtar*, which codified the myth of May's incompetence while backdating it to her prior productions. Even studio executives with whom May was not working directly did their part to turn industry sentiment against her. During the production of *A New Leaf*, for instance, Paramount executive Peter Bart made no secret about his feelings toward May: "I told [Robert] Evans and [Frank] Yablans that I didn't like or trust Elaine May and suspected that she didn't know which end of the camera to look through" (*Infamous Players* 145).

The combination of studio and journalistic interference has resulted in a strange paradox: a lack of wide popular awareness about May's work, despite her early fame, and an intense, almost worshipful appreciation of her genius among those in the know. Typical of the kind of gushing response the name "Elaine May" elicits among insiders is filmmaker Joan Darling's comment about why May could never serve as a feasible role model for other women: "[She] was such a complete auteur, I didn't think of her as just a director, I thought of her as a painter doing a whole painting" (qtd. in Gregory 33). More recently, May has garnered praise for her Tony-winning performance in Kenneth Lonergan's play *The Waverly Gallery*, which ran on Broadway in 2018 and 2019, and her surprise turn as Ruth Bader Ginsburg on the serial drama *The Good Fight*. To date, however, it is her creative partnership with Mike Nichols that remains the most well-documented aspect of her career, and at the time of writing, fans must still turn to Nichols's biography to learn more about May's. (This situation will be rectified in 2024 by the appearance of the first biography of May.[7]) Without begrudging Nichols his spotlight, too often May has been absorbed into her collaborators' legacies rather than given one of her own. It is not for nothing, after all, that May could joke at the 2010 American Film Institute event honoring Nichols about having worn the same dress to his "first" lifetime achievement award gala.[8] Meanwhile, in his history of American comedy, Gerald Nachman discusses Nichols's movie successes in detail over dozens of pages, while May's more eclectic postpartnership career merits the following synopsis: "a few acting jobs, screenplay doctoring . . . some movie directing . . . and the occasional play or screenplay, such as *Heaven Can Wait, A New Leaf* . . . and the landmark forty-million-dollar flop *Ishtar*, which entered the language as a synonym for disaster" (354).

What can get lost in this mixed or inconsistent messaging is that May is, simply, a major American artist, an originator of improv as we know it whose early collaboration with Nichols was immediately understood to have revolutionized comedy, and a creative multihyphenate who has influenced every medium she has worked in. A case could and probably should be more emphatically made for crediting May with inventing the "yes, and" rule and with helping to inaugurate the comic mode we now call "cringe," making her legacy broadly cultural as well as specifically cinematic. Indeed, it may be the very breadth of her accomplishments that has made them hard to categorize or fully recognize.

Recently, the critical tide has begun to turn, with May's cinema, in particular, becoming the subject of overdue reassessment. A small but growing body of scholarship, including a scholarly volume edited by Alexandra Heller-Nicholas and Dean Brandum, has begun to shed new light on May's multimedia body of work. In the last decade, a diverse group of film critics including Miriam Bale, Jonathan Rosenbaum, Richard Brody, and Manohla Dargis has helped to cultivate greater awareness and appreciation of May's films and nudged the much-maligned *Ishtar* closer to "cult" territory.[9] Indeed, there is the sense that at the time of this book's writing we are witnessing something like what *Sight and Sound* has called a "May Renaissance": the broader rediscovery of her work by a new generation of cinephiles, critics, and programmers, many of them "extremely online" and eager to share screenshots and GIFs from her films on Twitter or to "clap back" at haters.[10] Earlier this year, film critic Jordain Searles, asked on social media to offer appraisals of given directors, said of May: "She's a genius. She's one of our most underrated filmmakers. She's a living legend. She's basically made only classics. One of the greatest to ever do it." Recently, the film journal *Bright Wall/Dark Room* devoted a special issue to May's career, and several podcasts have similarly dedicated series to her cinema. Established institutions seem to share this enthusiasm: New York repertory house Film Forum programmed a 2019 retrospective of May's films, while the Criterion Collection released *Mikey and Nicky*, the first (and to date only) of May's films to get the kind of prestige treatment generally reserved for venerated auteurs. In 2013 President Barack Obama awarded May a National Medal of Arts; in 2016 the Writers Guild of America granted her its Laurel Award for Screenwriting Achievement; and in 2022 she was granted an honorary Oscar. May, in short, is having a moment.

Making a case for May's auteur status, however, also entails the recognition of auteurism's limitations and its historically fraught politics for women filmmakers in particular.[11] Practically speaking, the fact that May's career was prematurely curtailed means that she—like many female directors of her era—does not have a filmography comparable in scope to that of her male contemporaries. Unfortunately, when it comes to auteurist assessments, size *does* matter. At the same time, her well-documented struggles with studio executives during the production and editing of her films deprived her of the degree of creative latitude enjoyed by many of her peers and celebrated by pop historians such as Peter Biskind who have helped memorialize the New Hollywood era as one of unfettered freedom—for the lucky few. As Haskell writes of the period's marquee directors, "It is to take nothing away from their achievements to remark that it"—New Hollywood—"was mostly a dude thing" ("Mad Housewives" 18). May's case, then, represents just one argument in favor of embracing what Kyle Stevens has called a "mutable" concept of authorial signature so as to account for more intermittent or incomplete expressions of directorial style (*Mike Nichols* 26).[12] In an industry in which women filmmakers have both been granted fewer opportunities to work and enjoyed less complete control over the final results when they do, it is arguably essential to recalibrate our critical understanding of what counts as a signature—that is, what aesthetic, narrative, or ideological traces may be less detectable to an interpretive apparatus optimized for totalizing displays of authorship over a sustained run of feature-length films.

In this sense, auteurism raises philosophical as well as practical questions, especially for feminist critics who have long viewed auteurist frameworks as "incorrigibly compromised," given their role in perpetuating a disproportionately male canon (Paszkiewicz 5). As Jessica Ford succinctly describes the feminist dilemma, "To absorb women directors into a discourse of auteurism is to ignore the embedded problems with this discourse" (22). Reservations notwithstanding, there remain compelling reasons for claiming female auteurs, not least of which is the visibility such exposure affords—as evidenced by director-centric series such as the one in which this book appears. Even a resolute antiauteurist such as Angela Martin concedes, citing the work of Carrie Tarr, that scholars have made a persuasive case for the "political necessity for defending female authorship as a useful and necessary category" (Carrie Tarr, qtd. in Martin 30). Even more compelling, however, may be the benefits of recuperating the notion of creative agency, an approach advocated by scholars such as Catherine Grant and Katyryzna Pasckiewicz, which allows scholars to account for the many industrial, cultural, and historical circumstances that have inflected women's labor in cinema. This "contextual turn" in feminist authorship studies is one I embrace in this book, and it is a necessity for evaluations of May's work, given how frequent, intense, and particular were the obstacles she faced as a woman director in 1970s and 1980s Hollywood.

May and Feminism

May herself had little interest in the feminist movement. Asked about feminism or her experience of gender discrimination directly, she tends to deflect or obfuscate, as she does in this faux interview with playwright and director Kenneth Lonergan: "I am one hundred percent in favor of feminism as long as it falls under the umbrella of humanism," she writes in a ventriloquized male voice, "which to me is the really important thing" (May, "Elaine May Interviews"). Despite her lack of avowed investment in feminist politics, however, it is difficult to deny the salience of gender both to the contemporary reception of May's films and to their revaluation by a younger generation of viewers.[13] However disinclined May herself has been to claim the label of feminist—a position she shares with more experimental directors of the era Chantal Akerman—she is clearly cognizant of gender's impact on her career. As she noted drily in one interview, "Clint Eastwood I think could do anything because he's tall and they respect him, and in that way it is better to be Clint Eastwood than a woman in Hollywood" (Guest, postscreening discussion about *Ishtar*).

This double standard becomes more clearly present in press coverage, which reveals how reflexively auteurism was weaponized against May. She was taken to task for precisely the kinds of behaviors and tendencies (perfectionism, obsessiveness) frequently celebrated when associated with male auteurs such as Stanley Kubrick and Alfred Hitchcock—or, closer to home, her collaborator Warren Beatty. By the time May began shooting *Ishtar*, she was too big *not* to fail: in possession of too strong a sensibility, too large a budget, and too irreverent an attitude toward Hollywood's stars and shibboleths to escape the opprobrium of studio executives and critics whose expectations about female directors she apparently defied. As May herself put it, "People would leave me saying, she's a nice girl . . . and the thing is, of course, I wasn't a nice girl. And when they found this out, they hated me all the more" ("Elaine May in Conversation").

May also drew fire from women—principally, the feminist critics whose responses to her work ranged from ambivalent to openly hostile. Barbara Quart was among her films' most vocal opponents, advancing the line that May "aims a particular animus at her women characters and works through male protagonists" (37). Indeed, May's tendency to center men more than women was definitive in ensuring that May was never "neatly legible as a feminist" (Hastie 192). Yet if Quart got some things exactly right—that May "has always worked through genre forms," for instance, or the "extent to which [hers] is a world of continual betrayal"—other assertions appear by turns uncharitable, wrongheaded, or both, to wit, her contention that May turned, after her partnership with Nichols, to "an unsuccessful attempt at playwriting and an equally unsuccessful marriage" (40). Quart's readings of May's films seem particularly tendentious in their insistence on minimizing May's comic mandate ("granted, comedy has to make fun of people") in order to read antifeminist intent into *A New Leaf* and *The Heartbreak Kid* (42). She argues of both that "the female portraits here run a singularly demeaning range" and that the latter film, especially, produces "one of the most negative images of a Jewish woman on film" (Quart 42). Molly Haskell initially concurred, arguing in *From Reverence to Rape: The Treatment of Women in the Movies* that May's films "inarguably contain some of the most gratuitously nasty images of women to appear in the last ten years" (376). But she has since revised her take, remarking in a 2019 essay that May "cast a gimlet eye on masculine entitlement and bravado in [her] wonderfully idiosyncratic comedies" (22).[14]

The degree of vitriol originally directed at May by feminist critics might seem puzzling to present-day viewers, given the evident pleasure her films take in deflating the male ego. As Miriam Bale put it in a now-deleted social media survey of directorial obsessions, May had a fetish for "dumb men." Yet as Maggie Hennefeld has pointed out, "Feminism has always had an uneasy relationship with comedy," a tension she attributes in part to its "anti-laughter ethos, inherited from the anti-pleasure polemics of second wave feminism" (6, 5). May, in other words, was making tactical use of cinema's pleasures at the very moment when feminist theorists such as Laura Mulvey were calling for their "destruction." Moreover, as scholars such as Smukler point out, women's scant numbers in 1970s Hollywood meant that each "automatically carried the burden of representing all women directors," making May's perceived transgressions all the more objectionable (*Liberating Hollywood* 86).

In particular, it's clear that May's movies presented a "positive images" problem (Haskell, "Mad Housewives" 25). Not only did they feature passive, painfully awkward, or even abject female characters such as Henrietta in *A New Leaf* and Lila in *The Heartbreak Kid*—hardly "strong" female role models—but they also centered male perspectives and deprioritized female ones at a moment when representation was seen as an index of ideology and avenue for revision. Similarly, as Quart points out, May took a "broader, unashamedly popular road" at a time when many of the most acclaimed women directors were coming through "the non-commercial route of independent cinema" (39). The result was that May's commercial efforts were not received as "redemptive texts," despite the fact that their subversive qualities are not exactly concealed (Hennefeld 34).

Ultimately, it seems fair to speculate that if May's films didn't register at the moment of their release as "positive examples," it might have more to do with the contexts of reception than with qualities or lacunae within the films themselves (Hennefeld 34).[15] In other words, the outsized expectations placed on women directors may have prevented viewers from recognizing in May's images of immiserated women "an objective correlative to the patriarchal attitudes that subordinate [women] in real life"—that is, from seeing these portrayals as a pointed tactic rather than a misstep (Morrison 122).

Significantly, the methods that proved so alienating to some second-wave feminist viewers appear more legible to a newer generation, which recognizes that "negative" portrayals of women notwithstanding, May's cockeyed comedies also offer some of the sharpest takes on sexual politics in postclassical American cinema. As Elise Moore notes in a recent issue of *Bright Wall/Dark Room*, "May is interested in misogyny the way Hitchcock is interested in murder: she wants to know what it is like, not moralize about it." Such criticism understands May's focus on men as strategic. Or, put another way, her films focus on men but aren't *focalized* through them; instead, her movies maintain a studied detachment from any single character's point of view, a mode of subtle distanciation that becomes one of the primary and implicitly modernist mechanisms through which May defamiliarizes the specific forms of gendered cruelty on display. If *The Heartbreak Kid* and *A New Leaf*, for instance, don't resort to the more emphatic alienation tactics of other feminist films of the era—the granular realism of *Wanda* (1970) or the extreme duration of *Jeanne Dielman, 23, quai du Commerce, 1080 Bruxelles* (1975)—it is difficult to watch May's films and not discern in her dialogue, framing, editing, and mise-en-scène that she has arranged all the resources at her disposal to expose masculinity's self-regard in its unflattering particulars. Of course, as Moore concedes, "It's not as though her women represent an attractive alternative position for the viewer to occupy." But the absence of *any* comfortable vantage point—of an "attractive" position for viewing—is precisely the point, forcing viewers to reconsider the default expectations of film spectatorship.

As sui generis as May's corpus of films may be, the trajectory of her career—especially its premature curtailment—remains a depressingly common one for female directors. If in the 1970s May was only the third woman to have been inducted into the Directors Guild of America, in the 2000s the #TimesUp and #MeToo movements have made it clear that the odds against women filmmakers' success in Hollywood, while certainly improved, are still far from equitable.[16] In this sense, as the final section discusses, May is at once utterly exceptional and completely exemplary.

"Born in a Trunk": The Perils of Biography

If auteurist and feminist approaches yield insights into May's cinema, biography has proved both a more common and a less elucidating lens for discussing her work. A critical survey of secondhand accounts reveals how often assessments of May's behavior have superseded analyses of her art, a finding that raises larger questions about the limits of biographical criticism. What happens, in other words, when we free May from what the writer Milan Kundera calls the *"mini-mini-mini context"* of biography—an approach to which minoritized artists may be particularly susceptible—and reinsert her into the mainstream of film history (269)? What do we discover when we situate May's films within the full arc of a career that has encompassed major achievements as a comedian, playwright, screenwriter, and actor and treat her own body of work as an essential intertext for her films?

According to the biographical précis that is most often reproduced in both popular and scholarly accounts of May, she was born Elaine Iva Berlin in 1932 to the actors Ida and Jack Berlin in Philadelphia. Beginning at a young age, she performed with her father in a Yiddish theater company, leading an itinerant life on the road, at least until her father's death prompted May and her mother's relocation to Los Angeles. "By the time she was ten," one *Life* interviewer reported, "she had been in more than fifty schools, some for only a few weeks at a time" (Thompson 37). As May put it, "I kept learning that Mesopotamia was the first city. I also frequently learned the multiplication tables up to five" (qtd. in Thompson 37). Not surprisingly, she developed a dim view of formal education and left school permanently at fourteen. She married at sixteen and gave birth to her daughter at seventeen. Several years later, in 1955, she lit out for Chicago, where she met Nichols and audited classes at the University of Chicago. She also helped found the nation's first improvisational comedy theater, the Compass Players—which would subsequently pave the way for The Second City—and, together with Nichols, traveled to New York, where the two helped to revolutionize American comedy. The rest is theater (and film) history.

Yet as some commentators have pointed out, the details included in this origin story are hardly established fact.[17] Indeed, May herself disowned this account in a 2010 conversation with Jonathan Rosenbaum, countering that she was actually born in Chicago. As Rosenbaum reports, "May told me at our June 27 meeting that much of the biographical information that circulates about her is false, mainly due to her own idle inventions to the press over the years. She said that she was actually born in Chicago, and further suggested that the story about her growing up in the Yiddish theatre was not strictly accurate." A more recent conversation with May's close collaborator and friend Julian Schlossberg, however, reaffirmed the original version, that May's birth place is very likely Philadelphia, underscoring the persistent uncertainty around her origins.[18] At other points, she has disowned any account, famously writing, in place of a biographical statement on her 1959 album with Nichols, *Improvisations to Music*, that "Miss May does not exist." Later events in May's life are somewhat easier to confirm. Married three times—including, briefly, to *Fiddler on the Roof* lyricist Sheldon Harnick—she later enjoyed a twenty-year partnership with Stanley Donen, who by all accounts proposed to her "about 172 times" (Donen died in 2019) (Heilpern). Today, May lives in the same apartment building as her daughter, actor Jeannie Berlin, on New York's Upper West Side. But May's aversion to the press ensures that a certain mystery remains, reflected in the comically vague coda that concludes her bio in *The Waverly Gallery* playbill: "She has done more but this is enough."

The prevailing narrative of May's early life as bohemian nomad—"born in a trunk," to quote a Compass Players colleague (qtd. in Coleman 68)—has the advantage of affirming certain widespread and rather romantic preconceptions about May's outsider status, grounding in

Jewish comedy, and theatrical bona fides. The absence of additional information or firsthand confirmation from the intensely private May, however, means that even the most conscientious accounts of her life risk overindexing what could be apocrypha or at the very least half-truths. In fact, the consequences of May's reticence reflect yet another of the double standards she has had to contend with. While male artists seemingly enjoy the right to privacy, women who elect anonymity have not been granted similar license. The result is that the silence of a Thomas Pynchon or a Stanley Kubrick is respected, for instance, while May's silence—or, in a different field, that of the novelist Elena Ferrante—is not. Indeed, one might look at the attempted "outing" of Ferrante, whose clear-eyed studies of male self-regard share some thematic territory with May's, as proof that coerced transparency can conceal misogynistic intent.[19] Repeatedly, interviews and other coverage of May reveal resentment at her perceived "spectrality" (O'Farrell). During one of May's rare public appearances at the New School in 1975, for instance, the interviewer began by commenting to his guest that "she seemed to spend much of her life hiding." "Well, I don't know why I should reveal myself to you," May responded. "After all, we've only known each other about an hour. What do you want to know?" (qtd. in Rivlin 81).[20]

If details of May's early life remain unverified, accounts of her professional career can, by contrast, appear overdetermined. Janet Coleman's history of the Compass Players, for instance, quotes a long list of fellow (male) performers whose highly positive assessments of May's intellect and creative brilliance are accompanied by equally gushing endorsements of her sex appeal and colored by what many concede were feelings of envy or lust. Two unassailable facts emerge most clearly from the accounts reproduced in both Coleman's book and Mark Harris's biography of Mike Nichols: May was widely understood by her contemporaries (and successors) to be a genius; and, partly as a result, May consistently inspired both admiration and anxiety among her male colleagues, whose enthusiasm for her work was tempered by professional and sexual jealousy. Omar Shapli, for one, recalled May's "piercing, dark-eyed, sultry stare": "It was really unnerving. . . . She was like Carmen. She seemed like a potential black widow" (qtd. in Coleman 66). Tom O'Horgon and Martin Peiser were similarly awed, calling May a "scarifying lady" and a "maninizer," respectively, while ex-boyfriend James Sacks waxed rhapsodically (and condescendingly) about her "beautiful raw madness" and "raw unpolished intelligence" (66). Bob Smith's crude comments, however, may be most revealing of the extent to which May was subject to both objectification and idolatry: "She had the darkest smoldering eyes and the biggest tits I've ever seen" (66).

What's troubling, of course, is that the image of May as "maninizer" that emerges from such secondhand reports risks obscuring the reality of May as triple threat, a supremely talented writer, actor, and director for stage and screen.[21] When critic Edmund Wilson confessed in his memoirs, "I've always been such easy game for beautiful, gifted women, and [Elaine] is the most so I've seen since Mary McCarthy in the thirties," he seemingly couldn't help but follow it up with a crude and sexist coda: "I imagine that she, too, would be rough-going" (39). To read the accounts of May furnished by men in her professional orbit, in short, is to confront precisely the displays of male ego that would feature in her films. In his biography of Nichols, Mark Harris identifies this dynamic and its material consequences. As he observes, during her time with the Compass Players, May was "one of the few performers who could not only act and direct but write. Time and again she would save [the group]" by furnishing them with material, but "they could barely bring themselves to thank her" (Harris 51). It's an account corroborated by May's Compass colleague Mark Gordon: "Somebody maybe would say, 'Oh I guess it's all right.' But there was never a recognition that Elaine's stuff was fantastic" (qtd. in Harris 51). Other former Compass Players confirm that "her scenarios were routinely savaged by the other members of the cast" (Coleman 145). Roger Brown recalled one instance in which "Elaine felt we had made a travesty of her idea. There was a display of anger. And we, being men, just ignored her. Nothing new about that" (qtd. in Coleman 109).

It may not be surprising to learn, in this light, that some of the more substantive insights into May's work and sensibility come from the women she collaborated with earlier in her career. One particularly suggestive comment comes from Compass Players member Annette Hankin, a former mentee of May's who remarked on the energy May "spent defending herself": "She was one of those women who perceives herself as feeling very vulnerable. In fact, she was one of the toughest women I ever knew, a real tough cookie. It came from some perception that she had to defend herself in a world that would eat her alive. The heroines of her plays are always very vulnerable people who are eaten alive" (qtd. in Coleman 111–12). What makes the combination of toughness and vulnerability that Hankin discerns in May less paradoxical, however, is the fact that May, by all accounts, *did* have to defend herself in the sense that she was regularly forced to deflect all manner of unwelcome or unreciprocated advances. As Mark Harris reports, "Many of the men she worked with wanted her, something she had learned to navigate in a way that would preserve her growing status without demolishing guys who could then punish her for rejecting them" (50). Or as May apparently said to the novelist Herbert Gold, who briefly dated her, "If I kiss, I fuck, and I don't want to fuck" (qtd. in Nachman 329). If the female characters in May's films are less adept at self-defense than their author, it may be by design, since their helplessness throws into relief the forms of aggression, and passive aggression, that made her own maneuvers necessary. May's heroines—the hapless Henrietta (*A New Leaf*), naïve Lila (*The Heartbreak Kid*), and fragile, exploitable Nell (*Mikey and Nicky*)—may be frustrating in their defenselessness. Then again, it is their susceptibility to mistreatment that allows May to showcase it: to dramatize the "outrages perpetrated against vulnerable women," as Coleman wrote of May's theatrical work, "by their mothers and men" (11).

Men Explain Things to May

May has been the subject not just of one-sided characterizations by colleagues but also of inaccurate and at times openly sexist treatment by the press. Such sensationalized coverage reached its apex during the release of *Ishtar*, epitomized by the breathless cover story David Blum wrote for *New York* magazine about the film's production, discussed in greater detail below. Even before the media helped legitimize such "industry lore," however, May had long privately contended with concerns regarding her perceived unruliness.[22] An early profile in the *New Yorker*, for instance, recounts the attempts of Nichols and May's manager, Alexander H. Cohen, "to reshape Miss May into the model of efficiency he thought at first she should be": "He laid out a complete daily schedule for her, reproved her for neglecting a number of chores she had undertaken to do, and gave her various pieces of avuncular advice about how to live her life" (Rice 72). Even if Cohen ultimately realized his error, some of May's closest collaborators still succumbed to a similar temptation to "reshape" or "improve" her. Nichols himself has admitted that he was not exempt from this behavior and has confessed that as their live comedy show continued, he began "to be a real pain in the ass to her. I was very controlling—'You were a little too slow tonight'" (qtd. in Harris 109). It got to the point that he "would stand in the wings, gesturing at her to move it along" (109).[23] Journalists, quick to seize on May's career missteps, have often amplified this impression of her helplessness and dependence on male peers. Thus, a profile in *Life* magazine detailing May's collaboration with Carl Reiner on his 1967 film *Enter Laughing* described the director as "an unlikely shepherd [who] led Elaine out of the valley of professional darkness" (Thompson 43).

Significantly, May took up this characterization of her own shortcomings in her films, particularly in her first two movies, which feature women being chastised by disapproving male partners for precisely those behaviors—slowness, slovenliness—anecdotally attributed to their creator. In *The Heartbreak Kid*, for instance, the heroine, Lila, is continually hurried by her manic husband.[24] In *A New Leaf*, meanwhile, the character of Henrietta, played by May herself, is defined by her klutziness: she spills food and drink, can't keep her glasses on or her clothes straight, and needs to be continually decrumbed. (As Walter Matthau's character complains, "She has to be vacuumed every time she eats!") Many of the character's mannerisms feature in accounts of May herself. Compass Players performer Barbara Harris, for instance, describes May as "so . . . well . . . incompetent in terms of being able to get her clothes on," while others reported of May that "little scraps of paper trailed her. She was always dropping things" (qtd. in Coleman 68, 67).

In short, May's perceived inefficiencies—personal and creative—were a source of speculation, if not consternation, long before she started directing. That she chose to dramatize these same inefficiencies within her films and to make them the subject of comedy did not also prevent the discourse of May's "difficulty" from gaining credence and, eventually, being leveraged against her by critics and studio heads who were more disposed toward a story of female incompetence than of female brilliance thwarted. Perhaps the best that can be said of the ad hominem attacks is that they serve to expose the unspoken biases that have too often shaped popular perceptions of female artists.

"Take the Unlikely Choice": The Legacy of Improv

Compared to the variously reliable anecdotes furnished by others, May's own body of work provides a rich and compelling framework for considering her cinema. Among the most widely appreciated of May's accomplishments remains the improvised comedy she performed with Nichols in the late 1950s and early 1960s. Shortly after the two arrived in New York from Chicago in 1958, they attracted an agent, Jack Rollins, who helped turn the two young performers into sensations almost literally overnight. The sketches they created and performed together as Nichols and May led to three comedy albums, *Improvisations to Music* (1958), *An Evening with Mike Nichols and Elaine May* (1960), and the Grammy-nominated *Mike Nichols and Elaine May Examine Doctors* (1962). The second album immortalized the premiere of their Broadway show of the same name, which ran for nine months and 311 performances before May decided to end its run and with it the couple's professional partnership (Harris 100, 110). While the pair would periodically reunite—for TV appearances on *The Jack Paar Show* and JFK's birthday celebration in 1962—they maintained their distance for decades. It was not until the 1990s that they resumed their collaboration. Within a few years, May would write the screenplay for two of Nichols's films, *The Birdcage* (1995) and *Primary Colors* (1998), and serve as an uncredited script doctor for a third, *Wolf* (1994). In 2010 May paid tribute to Nichols when he was granted an AFI Life Achievement Award and subsequently directed the *American Masters* documentary about his career, released in 2016, two years after his death.

Nichols and May's collaboration has had a lasting legacy. The two are widely credited, including by fellow comics, with having inaugurated a radically new mode of "intellectual" comedy and with setting new standards for dialogic realism in postwar American culture.[25] As Gerald Nachman puts it, they "established themselves as the leading social satirists of their generation, a title never seriously threatened in the forty years of sketch comedy since"; elsewhere, he credits them with inaugurating the "Age of Irony, later personified by comics like Steve Martin, Bill Murray, and David Letterman" (319, 323). At the same time, they were part of a generation exploring transformative new ideas about acting developed by Konstantin Stanislavski and disseminated in the United States by teachers such as Maria Ouspenskaya and Viola Spolin, with whom May and Nichols studied. Isaac Butler credits Nichols's early films, including *Who's Afraid of Virginia Woolf?* (1966) and *The Graduate* (1967), with popularizing Method approaches that have since become a dominant form of screen acting. But even in May and Nichols's earlier sketches—"Mother and Son," "Telephone Company Information Operators," "Name Dropping"—their close studies in human behavior were definitive in shaping the kind of socially observant comedy that has become pervasive. Comedians who have credited Nichols and May as an influence are legion and include everyone from Lily Tomlin, Jerry Seinfeld, and Nora Ephron to Patton Oswalt, Mindy Kaling, and John Mulaney.

Less well documented, however, is the formative influence of May's background in improvisational performance on her own filmmaking. While it's difficult to know how much improvisation survived in the final cuts of May's films, what is clear is that open-ended exploration constituted a crucial part of the rehearsal and production processes. In his memoir, for instance, Charles Grodin, who plays Lenny, shares details about May's direction on *The Heartbreak Kid*, a film that, despite its contractually mandated fidelity to Neil Simon's screenplay, was the product of extensive improvising on the set, much to Simon's dismay:

> When [Simon] attended our early rehearsals, and Elaine had Jeannie and me singing different songs that we might be singing as we drove to Florida on our honeymoon, Neil asked: "Where does it say they sing?" At the same time as he was understandably objecting to the improvising with which Elaine, Jeannie, and I were so comfortable, he also regarded Elaine so highly that a compromise was struck. We would film every word of the script exactly as written, and Elaine would be free to do whatever else she chose by way of improvisation, and then Elaine would put the film together. (191)[26]

Cybill Shepherd has similarly attested to May's use of improvisation during the film's production, which she at first found discomfiting: "This

Figure 2. *The Heartbreak Kid's*
singing newlyweds

was only my second film and I'd never taken acting lessons, so when she said, 'Let's improvise' I said: 'What's that?' It was so much fun, though. . . . Having Elaine as my first improv coach was such a blessing. She didn't try to dominate but she was always very specific about what she wanted" (qtd. in Gilbey). Walter Matthau, by all accounts, was less sanguine about May's improvisational approach and being asked to submit to "as many as twenty takes," calling May, "lovingly, Mrs. Hitler" (Wasson 151). But it was costume designer Anthea Sylbert, not May's actors, who may have offered the most incisive commentary on her methods: "Elaine does [all those takes] because she's looking for something other than that which is presented" (qtd. in Wasson 151).

Even more suggestive, perhaps, was the improvisation that evidently took place on the *Mikey and Nicky* shoot. While May's producers and collaborators have corrected the impression that the film was improvised, it's nonetheless clear that a great deal of exploration occurred during rehearsals—many of them filmed—and at times created consternation among crew members and even May herself. At one point, evidently feeling that John Cassavetes, who stars as Nicky, had wandered too far afield during his scenes, May had her assistant slip a note under his door that read, "Elaine says learn the lines" (Canford 75). Then again, May's own directing methods owed something to her training in improv. Desirous of eliciting a more enraged reaction from Peter Falk, who plays Mikey, May apparently directed his scene partner to deliver the wrong lines; at another point, she closed a door that should have been opened, angering Cassavetes. Then there was the moment when, by Falk's account, she called him aside while filming a particularly intense scene to offer what he expected would be a valuable note. Instead, she bit him on the lip—as the character played by Carol Grace was required to do in the scene—prompting what Falk describes as a phenomenal take: "[Did] that scene sing. What a take! I loved it. . . . I still didn't fully comprehend what had just happened. I just remember feeling good—elated—and in awe of what Elaine had done" (*Just One More Thing* 228).

Of particular interest in assessing the impact of May's theatrical training on her filmmaking are the principles of improvisation that she, together with Ted Flicker, would help enumerate during the summer of 1957. The resulting list, which codifies "The Rules" for successful improv, included some already in de facto use by the Compass Players: "(1) whatever verbal or pantomimed reality that is brought to the stage by one player may not be negated or denied by the other; (2) while improvising, a player has infinite opportunities for choice, and it is better to take an active than a passive choice ('take the unlikely choice,' Del Close recalls as a phrase of Elaine's); and (3) in an improvisation, where there are no lines, or given actions, or dramaturgical 'spine' to a set character in motion, *you* are your character, although not one called by your name" (Coleman 226). If the first rule has in time become the most famous—often invoked as the "yes, and" rule of improv, which requires buying into your partner's proposed reality—the second may be just as relevant for understanding May's cinema.[27] The preference for the "unlikely choice" that Del Close attributed to May is especially salient and, according to Compass Players colleagues, shaped May's own approach to live performance: "Whenever [Nichols] would go for a joke, she would do something unexpected, throw him off balance, side-skirt him" (qtd. in Coleman 167). May, significantly, has demonstrated a similar predilection for the unexpected in her private dealings as well as her public performances, especially in interviews, where she frequently upends the expectations of the genre. Concluding one rather perfunctory interview with Richard Shepherd in the *New York Times*, for instance, she replied to the interviewer's word of thanks by saying, "Maybe you're welcome" (qtd. in Kapsis 20). This "unlikely" qualification of linguistic formula is consonant with her films' tendency to thwart visual or generic expectations, which is to say, to resist cliché and "boredom" at all costs. As May once put it, "To actually make something that isn't boring is sort of hard to do" (Probst 133). Years later, Carly Simon would immortalize May's apparent allergy to boredom in a conversation with Charlie Rose: "I've got a friend who is so afraid of boredom she actually faints after a minute of being bored at a party. She just faints, and then she spends the rest of the party under the table." "Who is that?" Rose probes. "Elaine May . . . I probably shouldn't . . . Oh God, Elaine, forgive me!"

"Step by Tiny Step": May's Comic Incrementalism

Especially notable is how closely the "rules" May helped to outline parallel her avowed theory of comedy, which, in turn, would clearly inform her feature films. As she put it, "Comedy is almost entirely the doing of something in detail, step by tiny step. Drama sort of sweeps everything away" (Probst 135). This kind of comic incrementalism, as May describes it, has considerable explanatory power when applied to both her films and her early sketches with Nichols. Just as Nichols and May's improvised scenes often entailed dilating on a premise—a phone call, a hospital visit, a first date—"step by tiny step," her films contain episodes that not only feel as though they could stand alone as comic routines but also appear, in their carefully paced but continually escalating absurdism, to be structured according to the constraint of "yes, and." Indeed, one could argue that all her movies proceed by methodically taking a far-fetched conceit to its logical (or illogical) conclusion: a man plans to marry and kill a rich heiress for money (*A New Leaf*), a newlywed jilts his wife on their honeymoon (*The Heartbreak Kid*), a low-level gangster helps an incompetent hit man assassinate his childhood friend (*Mikey and Nicky*), two hack musicians get caught up in geopolitical intrigue in the Middle East (*Ishtar*). As Kyle Stevens has observed, *A New Leaf* is essentially a two-hour-long answer to the question, "What . . . might [it] *really* look like for a man to be willing to target, marry, and kill a woman for money[?]" ("Elaine May" 195). It's a setup that bears a strong similarity to the one May has provided by way of illustrating her comic method:

You can do something dramatically or you can do it funny. You can kill somebody dramatically or you can kill them funny. Funny is closer to life. If you kill somebody in a drama you get a gun and shoot them and they die, and then you're left to face the consequences of your act. If you kill somebody in a comedy you have to start out by finding a place where you can buy a gun that can't be traced. Or you have to buy a gun and then spend your evenings and weekends filing off the serial number. Then you have to buy cartridges. Then you have to learn how to load the gun and fire it. Then you have to put the gun and cartridges somewhere where they won't be found by the maid or your wife. Then when the time comes you have to get the guy you're going to kill either to come up to your apartment or make a date to meet him some place where you can fire a gun and no one will notice. Like Central Park. (qtd. in Probst 134–35)

May goes on at some length. Following her line of thought suggests that what has often been construed (and criticized) as May's perfectionism might more accurately be understood as *proceduralism*. She revisited the idea in a more recent discussion at the Harvard Film Archive, noting that "most comedies really have to do with what can go wrong" (see the next section, "An Interview with Elaine May"). In response to a follow-up question about the lackluster nature of Hollywood comedy, she added, "The kind of comedy that would be like stand-up is just detail. *The real truth, the real observation, of how difficult it is to get anything done*" (see the next section, "An Interview with Elaine May," italics mine).

One interesting by-product of May's step-by-step approach is that it can lead to a disorienting lack of narrative perspective, with the telos of a particular scene—Henry Graham's lawyer's attempt to inform his client that he's broke, or Mikey's efforts to coax his friend Nicky out of a hotel room—continually deferred, the "point" nearly lost in the shuffle of accumulating comic beats and gestures. Pauline Kael would implicitly take May to task for this quality in her review of *Such Good Friends* (1971), describing the film—whose screenplay May helped to author pseudonymously—as "all peripheral" ("Pleasing" 78). Nichols and others have offered similar criticisms, suggesting that if May was a seemingly inexhaustible source of new material, someone else was required to shape it, to give it purpose and structure.[28] As Janet Coleman put it, "She was interested in character and the moment. [Nichols] was interested in moving on" (131). Nichols himself has said much the same thing: "I was always very concerned with beginning, middle, and end, and when it's time for the next point . . . she had endless capacity for invention. My invention was not endless. . . . [S]he was a much better actor than I was. She could go on and on in a character. I could not. I had to move on to the next point because I was out. I couldn't do any more" (qtd. in Coleman 131).

Edmund Wilson, an ardent fan of May's, critiqued her on a similar count, noting that "she had no sense of form . . . but would go on and on in their dialogues," a point on which Nichols and May's manager, Jack Rollins, essentially concurred: "Elaine would go on forever if you let her. She is insanely creative, but she had no sense when to quit" (174, qtd. in Nachman 342). If this tendency is portrayed as a shortcoming, however, the shapelessness that was the perceived by-product of May's "endless" invention might just as easily be understood as a gift, the natural expression of her commitment "to find[ing] the truth of a moment improvisationally" (Coleman 72). As some critics have recently noted, the problem is not May's methods so much as her historical moment: the fact that she was "simply a searcher . . . an explorer born too far ahead of the equipment required for her success" (Carlin). In other words, May's openness to chance—her willingness to "go on and on" both as a director and as an actor—would be better tolerated in the digital era, in which such exploration doesn't necessarily come at practical expense. "In the age of mumblecore and digital filmmaking," Matt Carlin writes, "the idea of keeping the camera running and searching for, if not truth, then at least comedy, is common. After all, there is no film being burnt." From this vantage point, the "endless" or inexhaustible dimension of May's approach is more readily recovered as a feature of her filmmaking rather than a bug—a reflection of her desire to get "closer to life."

"Imagine Not Knowing": May's Theater of the Real-Life Absurd

Compared to the comedy she performed with others, May's individually authored work as a playwright remains far less examined. This may in large part be a function of access: it remains difficult to obtain copies of May's published scripts, many of which are only available for purchase through specialized websites. (There are reviews of the plays' productions but little scholarly discussion of the scripts themselves.) But there has also been a perception of her plays as existing "apart" from her cinema; as Rosenbaum remarks in a piece on May's writing and directing for film, "Her plays for the stage are perhaps another matter and won't be dealt with here" (365). If it's true that her work as a playwright has not to date figured in most critical discussions of her films—and that a number of her scripts were completed in the years after her directorial career—then May's plays are, in fact, an immensely valuable resource for thinking and theorizing about her cinema.

On the whole, her work for stage and screen is strikingly unified in its thematic focus on men (and occasionally women) struggling against the tide of their own lives and the extravagant difficulty such efforts entail. (In some cases, the continuities within her multimedia corpus are material; for instance, the screenplay for *Mikey and Nicky* originated as the script for a play.[29]) Written between 1962 and 2011, May's twelve plays center around characters operating under the particularly American delusion that the straitjackets of circumstance or social convention might, through sheer force of will, be escaped. There's an escalating tension, then, between the progressively manic behavior and outsized ambitions of her characters and the generally unresponsive nature of their surroundings. The result is farce, but shot through with a certain sardonic realism.

Her first play, the off-Broadway hit *Adaptation* (1968), provides a bracing example of broad conceit used as a vehicle for social commentary. The play envisions life as a running game show: the main character and "contestant," Phil, gains and loses points as a commentator-cum-host assesses his fitful progress from infancy to adulthood. ("You have learned to Dissemble. Score two points for Maturity and advance to Public School" [May, *Adaptation* 8].) Phil seeks the elusive "Security Square"—not knowing, as the host has disclosed to the audience, that he could declare *any* square the definitive one and thus "win" the game at any point. Instead, Phil unwittingly pursues women, career success, and material wealth, even as he lies dying, in the last lines, of a coronary occlusion ("I wish I didn't have to quit so soon. If I could have played on a little while longer . . . " [30]). Within roughly thirty pages, May eviscerates the cruel optimism of "the simple American dream" (30) and the consequences of our collective acculturation—which is to say, our *adaptation*—to this ideological regime.[30]

In its coruscating portrait of postwar American life, *Adaptation* distills some of the key concerns of May's films, which similarly revolve around the spectacle of delusional male striving: the exertions of characters whose ambitions are generally in excess of their abilities. It's easy to see in Phil, for instance, an antecedent for *The Heartbreak Kid*'s Lenny Cantrow, whose frenzied attempts at assimilation achieve, in the end, less than nothing. While many of her plays, including *In and Out of the Light*, *Taller Than a Dwarf*, and *Adult Entertainment*, focus on ensembles and are somewhat broader in their satirical purview, her theatrical protagonists, like their analogues in May's films, are generally their own saboteurs, undone by unreasonable or unconscious desires. If Jean Renoir's poetic realism was defined by the humanist conviction that "everyone has their reasons," May's less sentimental vision seems to allow that everyone has, at best, *bad* reasons that may very well be unknown to the subjects themselves.[31]

Ignorance, in fact, is a nearly universal condition in May's plays. As in her films, characters in her plays are generally divided among those who don't know—May's "gallery of the oblivious," according to Brody— and those who *think* they do, creating a pervasive and often pleasurable sense of dramatic irony. In *Adaptation*, for instance, a running gag is that characters are blissfully unaware of their most obvious motives. Phil's mother tells his father shortly after giving birth:

> MOTHER: I am going to name him Phil. There's no reason for it. I just like the sound of the name.
> FATHER: It's a good name, Phyllis. (May, *Adaptation* 6)

The joke repeats later in the screenplay, suggesting that this kind of insensibility is pervasive. Even as May's characters cherish the illusion of their own agency (one could think of both *A New Leaf*'s Henry's and *The Heartbreak Kid*'s Lenny's increasingly frenzied attempts to secure fortunes and wives or the middle-aged dentist in *In and Out of the Light* chasing his buxom young assistant), their actions, to the audience, read as reactionary, driven more by social dogma than by self-determination. Even the intensely driven and utterly talentless musicians Lyle and Clark are motivated by a preformulated idea of "success" epitomized by the best-selling albums hanging in the window of Sam Goody's.

As if acknowledging the salience of the theme of blithe ignorance to her art, May's 2004 play, *Adult Entertainment*, includes some discussion of Gustave Flaubert's short story "Un coeur simple" ("A Simple Heart"), a text that reflects—like much of May's work—a gimlet eye for social bêtises. The play's ensemble, a group of porn actors who aspire to make a "real" movie, have been tasked by their pretentious director with reading the story in order to gain insight into "great literature." Having finished the Flaubert, one character offers her interpretation of the story's heroine, Félicité: "She goes to church and cleans and she keeps looking for people to love like they were her own but they never are. But what gets you is that she doesn't know. Her life is so bad before she gets hired as a maid that she thinks she's lucky" (May, *Adult Entertainment* 35). The other characters express incredulity at such a prospect:

JIMBO: Oh, wow. Imagine having a life like that and not knowing.
FROSTY MOONS: (*Slowly*) Yeah. Imagine not knowing. (36)

The joke, of course, is that these clueless characters *do* share Félicité's condition of "not knowing"—of thinking they're lucky, and lacking, much like *The Heartbreak Kid*'s Lila, *A New Leaf*'s Henrietta, or *Ishtar*'s Chuck and Lyle, the savvy to realize that they're not. *In the Spirit*, the 1990 independent film in which May costarred along with her daughter, Jeannie Berlin, riffs similarly on the human tendency to overestimate others' affection for them. "Of course, because you're my family!" one character exclaims. "I'm *Ed*'s family!" the other clarifies. Yet in many ways, the naïfs of May's fictions are better off than the alleged sophisticates, like the Yale-trained director Gerry in *Adult Entertainment* and Grodin's self-regarding CIA operative in *Ishtar*, who end up, for all their know-how, at a disadvantage. In May's universe, there are no real epiphanies, only false ones. Writing of Nichols and May's routines, Kyle Stevens has argued persuasively that "none of the characters can hear themselves, and so are unable to learn from each other" (*Mike Nichols* 50). It's a quality that persists in May's theater, in which such knowledge doesn't simply arrive too late; it doesn't arrive at all.

May's plays, moreover, feature in concentrated form her ear for the rhetoric of self-deceit and the forms of grandiloquence to which both her theatrical and her cinematic protagonists are similarly given. In *Taller*

Than a Dwarf, for instance, the main character, Howard, sounding like a bargain-basement Henry James, offers the following sub–*Beast in the Jungle*–style musings: "Last night I suddenly became aware that that thing, that special thing, I thought was going to happen to me—probably wouldn't and this was going to pretty much be it for the rest of my life" (May, *Taller* 8). Later, he pivots from self-aggrandizing reflection to self-pitying lament: "How did this happen? I did everything right. I was born white. I got good grades. And my life just feels . . . made-up, just meaningless, like something I'll do to pass the time until I die. I mean, don't you ever feel like that?" (21). Not for nothing are the protagonists of May's films given to similar flights of both self-pity and puffery. In *A New Leaf*, for instance, Henry Graham—shortly after discovering he has lost his fortune—makes a mock-tragic farewell tour of his luxe Manhattan haunts. May shoots his stops as a montage, overlaid with Henry's murmuring, in hushed voice-over, "I'm *poor*." Meanwhile, *The Heartbreak Kid*'s Lenny Cantrow, a Jewish interloper attempting to woo the staid Minnesotan parents of his would-be paramour, might be a Neil Simon creation, but his delivery channels the unfounded confidence of May's men, distilled in a ridiculous disquisition on the merits of midwestern food ("There's no deceit in the cauliflower"). In *Ishtar*, finally, nothing—not even the cold water thrown on their ambitions by their plain-speaking manager—can douse Lyle and Clark's conviction that they are, in fact, one hit song away from becoming the next Simon and Garfunkel. Is there anything heroic about being willing to blow up your lives for an ideal? It's a possibility that May's films *Ishtar* and *The Heartbreak Kid* and her plays *Taller Than a Dwarf* and *In and Out of the Light* toy with but never endorse.

Significantly, May's stage and screen characters are enabled in their delusion by others, as if even within the fictional world of the diegesis, subjects are bound by improv's mandate not to contradict another's verbal reality. For instance, May's early play *Not Enough Rope* (1964) depends on the willing participation of the protagonist's neighbors to assist with—or at least actively ignore—her plans for suicide, which she shares laughingly with a neighbor from whom she hopes to borrow some thicker rope: "I wanted to hang myself . . . but I don't know if twine would hold me . . . I'm kind of a heavy package" (6). Similarly, in *The Way of All Fish*, the rich employer appears to concede to the prospect of her own murder, while Shira Assel in *Ishtar* unquestioningly accepts Lyle and Clark's musical aspirations. Having established the absurd premise, May's plays proceed more or less matter-of-factly, the fictional world's plausibility enhanced by proliferating reality effects in the form of ethnic jokes, particularized mise-en-scènes, or characterizing mannerisms. Interestingly and perhaps not entirely incidentally, another author who surfaces as a point of reference in *Adult Entertainment* is Franz Kafka, a writer who, having required the reader to accept an implausible premise, tends to abide by the canons of realism. In the play, his name surfaces when the failed director, Gerry, defends the merits of reading "great writers": "It doesn't matter what they talk about. It's how they talk about it . . . how they lead you to the truth—*detail by detail, step by tiny step, until they break your heart, until their world is more real than your own*" (May, *Adult Entertainment* 56, italics mine). While Gerry is hardly a stand-in for May, it's fascinating to note that his thinking aligns so closely with May's own theory of comedy writing cited above. It's clear that May's theatrical scripts and cinematic screenplays reflect a shared commitment to proceeding "detail by detail, step by tiny step," creating entirely real worlds out of even the most seemingly absurd of scenarios.

Perhaps most significant, however, is that May's published scripts provide a forum for the more careful analysis of her dialogue-based humor. As a comic artist who makes extensive use of throwaway lines and what Kyle Stevens has called "dry" (as opposed to "wet") humor, which relies on active audience inference ("Politics"), the precision and complexity of May's language can readily be missed in a time-based medium like film, in which line readings are often downplayed and dialogue is casually tossed off. In *A New Leaf*, for instance, it is easy to miss lines like "Excuse me, you're not by any chance related to the Boston Hitlers?" or the devastating irony of the following exchange between Henrietta and her homicidal husband:

HENRIETTA: "I'm sorry to be so much trouble, dear."
HENRY: "Oh, it's alright, it isn't for long."

Studying May's plays and screenplays thus helps to codify her signature verbal tendencies. Of particular note is May's use of the "bad-to-worse" joke, in which the supposedly reassuring reply actually exacerbates rather than relieves discomfort. In such instances, the humor typically hinges on the invocation of mortality at a particularly inopportune time—when characters are especially demoralized, for instance, or least prepared to confront death. In *Taller Than a Dwarf*, for example, the married couple's dueling mothers nearly outdo themselves in delivering the punitive shtick Nichols and May had made famous in one of their best-known sketches, about guilt-inducing Jewish matriarchs, "Mother and Son." When the despondent Howard refuses to go to work, his mother intensifies the crisis by presenting him with an ultimatum: "You'll keep this job and you'll have a future and you'll be somebody if I have to drop dead in front of your eyes to make you do it!" (May, *Taller* 43). His mother-in-law, meanwhile, further ups the ante, putting him in mind of his *own* death: "What do you mean you quit. Are you crazy? You can't quit. When you die you'll quit" (53). This kind of perverse comic logic is commonplace in May's screenplays. It's particularly noticeable in the script she produced (uncredited) for *Such Good Friends*, in which the wife (played by Dyan Cannon) of a rapidly ailing patient fields a stream of faux-helpful comments from her husband's physicians: "Please try not to be bitter, there will be plenty of time for that later"; "Hospital care only really becomes adequate when a patient's life is in danger"; and, over a conversation in the hospital cafeteria, "Try the turkey [sandwich]. I promise you won't enjoy it." A variant on the false-comfort theme surfaces in *Ishtar*, when Lyle, while attempting to literally talk Chuck off a ledge, reminds him that circumstances could be even more desperate: "It takes a lot of nerve at your age to have nothing! You'd rather have nothing than settle for less."

These jokes reflect the fact that there's no real solace to be had in the universe of May's fictions, only the momentary comic relief that comes from realizing things could always be and likely *will* be worse. Even as her plays engage in absurdist logics, then, they don't allow for much "comic insulation," admitting real pathos—for the audience and characters—into cockeyed setups (Neale and Krutnik 69). It is no coincidence, and among the clearest evidence of May's debts to Jewish humor, that there is an ambient fatalism present across her plays, whose plots tend to feature murder (*The Way of All Fish*), suicide (*Not Enough Rope*, *Adult Entertainment*, *Hotline*), and premature death (*In and Out*

Figure 3. Artists out on the ledge:
a recurring trope

of the Light, Adaptation). Indeed, a recurring trope in May's work is that of the failed artist threatening to take their own life—Lyle the hack songwriter in *Ishtar* or the failed playwright in *Adult Entertainment*, who, during a crisis of self-doubt, also goes out on the window ledge. (Notably, a parallel scene plays out in *Luv*, a film starring May, which opens with the depressed Harry Berlin, played by Jack Lemmon, poised to leap from the Manhattan Bridge.)

In addition to her stage plays, May also wrote and rewrote an unknown number of film scripts. With rare exceptions, she did so pseudonymously or anonymously, rewriting the screenplay for *Such Good Friends* as Esther Dale and contributing to innumerable other films as an uncredited script doctor. (At one point, there were rumors that she, Joan Didion, and Griffin Dunne, among others, might create a script-doctoring collective.[32]) May has reportedly shaped films as diverse as *Reds* (1981), *Tootsie* (1982), *Labyrinth* (1986), *Wolf* (1994), *Ghostbusters II* (1986), and *Dangerous Minds* (1995), but, as Lindsay Zolandz writes, "It's impossible to say for sure how many famous scripts she's actually had an invisible hand in."[33] And, by some accounts, actually saved. Dustin Hoffman, for one, has been vocal in his praise for May's work on *Tootsie*, claiming, "Elaine is the one who made the movie work" (Rickey).[34] Among other changes, she apparently "gave it structure, created the Bill Murray character, wrote Hoffman's confessional monologue and deepened the female parts" (Rickey). It's worth noting that the screenplays for which she would accept credit—*Heaven Can Wait* (1978), *The Birdcage* (1996), and *Primary Colors* (1998)—are also those on which she collaborated with trusted partners such as Beatty and Nichols. (Two of those films, significantly, earned Oscar nominations.) Thus, while critics and interviewers have often expressed skepticism about May's preference for anonymity ("Don't you like credit?" Sam Kashner asked her during a 2013 conversation with Nichols for *Vanity Fair*), it's clear that she is only comfortable accepting it when she enjoys a high degree of creative control. In short, it's safe to say that, as Zolandz notes, "her impact is immeasurably wider" than she lets on. Or as May herself put it, "I do a lot of ghostwriting, which I can't talk about" (see the next section, "An Interview with Elaine May").

The result is that May completists may feel at times like they are playing an auteurist parlor game, attempting to "spot" her influence. In fact, what's striking is how clearly May's playful, ironic sensibility makes itself known within these work-for-hire projects—in the darkly comic dialogue of *Such Good Friends*, for instance, or the well-known scene from *Heaven Can Wait*, in which the butler explains the reason for the lady of the house's sudden scream: "[She] saw a mouse, but she's better now." "She just saw a mouse?" a guest asks, and the butler replies, "No, before, outside, but she relives it." Then there's the moment in *In the Spirit* (Sandra Seacat, 1990)—a movie May is rumored to have had a hand in shaping—when May's character turns to Marlo Thomas's to ask, in effect, about her imperviousness to irony: "Don't you know when people don't mean something?"[35] Even a film as seemingly distant from May's own oeuvre as Mike Nichols's *Wolf* (1994) features any number of lines that bear the trace of her influence. When Michelle Pfeiffer's character finds that her lover, played by Jack Nicholson, has handcuffed himself to prevent his lycanthropic transformation, she responds with exasperation that seems delightfully at odds with the film's urbane tone: "What was your plan, to sit chained to the radiator until you grew paws?" Any number of other lines suggest May's touch: "You are talking to an almost professional psychiatric nurse," "No, the worst things happen to the best people," "You're a nice person. Thank God I replaced you." At one point, we literally hear May's voice in the wake-up call Jack Nicholson's character requests from the hotel front desk. Then there is the scene in which Nicholson and Pfeiffer, playing members of New York's well-heeled elite, chew their way through peanut butter sandwiches—a very funny scene that seems to reflect May's predilection for putting glamorous stars into pedestrian setups.

Rather than artificially separate May's work for stage and screen, then, scholars are served by putting her contributions in both fields into greater proximity. Such juxtapositions are mutually illuminating, highlighting, for instance, the thematic parallels or dialogic tendencies that characterize her writing in both media. Such a move also strengthens the case for May's auteur status by attesting to the continuities of style and sensibility across these distinct art forms and fields of production.

May's Method

A final point of reference for approaching May's cinema and perhaps one most readily overlooked can be found in her turns acting in as well as writing and directing for film. With *A New Leaf*, May became only the second woman since Ida Lupino to write, direct, and star in a feature-length film for a major studio, but her screen appearances both preceded and succeeded this best-known performance. As an actor, her filmography encompasses early leading and supporting roles in mainstream comedies, including *Luv* (1967), *Enter Laughing* (1967), and *California Suite* (1978), as well as starring roles in independent films such as *In the Spirit* (1990)—cowritten by and costarring her daughter, Jeannie Berlin—and Woody Allen's *Small Time Crooks* (2000). She also costarred with Allen in the critically panned series he directed for Amazon, *Crisis in Six Scenes* (2016), and, more recently, continued her work for television with an appearance as Ruth Bader Ginsburg on an episode of Robert and Michelle King's show *The Good Fight* (2021). Her last film appearance, at the time of writing, was the 2021 film *The Same Storm*, directed by Peter Hedges. Dakota Johnson recently revived rumors that May is attached to direct her in a feature film called *Crackpot*, but there have been no developments since news of their collaboration first broke in 2019.

It is hard not to be struck by May's presence and incredible precision as a performer, her finely calibrated control of both voice and gesture. To watch May on-screen, in other words, is to watch her craft as well as her character; there is often a pleasurable consciousness of her artistry even as it functions simultaneously to conceal her art. A whole essay, for instance, could be written on May's voice to complement Alexandra Heller-Nichols's striking account of May's performative use of her hands ("In/Significant"). On-screen, that voice can range from the breathy and somewhat nasal—Marilyn Monroe by way of Brooklyn—which May channels for the charming ditzes she plays in *A New Leaf* and *Small Time Crooks*, to the deeper, more sultry tones she adopts for the jaded housewives in *Luv* and *California Suite*. In *Enter Laughing*, for instance, May plays a vampier Mrs. Robinson, batting her eyes and flirting with the young would-be actor who shows up in her dressing room. "I'm sure this isn't the first time you've been in a room with a girl who's dressing," she purrs as she puts on a pearl necklace over her black-lace negligée. The film appeared the same year as Nichols's *The Graduate* (1967), and it's hard not to notice the striking similarities between May's performance in this single scene—in which she rolls a beige stocking up one seductively posed leg—and Anne Bancroft's interpretation of a suburban seductress, who speaks in a similarly throaty contralto.

More recently, in Woody Allen's Amazon series *Crisis in Six Scenes*, May's hesitant line readings bring a level of pathos and sincerity into what would otherwise feel like stock farce. Addressing Allen, typecast as the show's neurotic protagonist, she says, "You know, we just drag

Figure 4. May in *Enter Laughing*: shades of
Mrs. Robinson

around in this everyday marriage, and I just thought . . . this is something so different" (season 1, episode 5, 13:55).[36]

May's performance throughout the series exemplifies the "improvisational" style of screen acting that James Naremore has, in fact, traced back to Nichols and May's comedy, in which actors "rely on naturalistic clumsiness—a halting, nervous incoherence, together with little indications of tension and repression. Their style is less presentational, less clearly enunciated than any comedy in history, more given to free-associational monologues, quick, overlapping responses, and apparently extemporaneous outbursts of emotion" (Naremore 281–82). Watch a routine like "Water Cooler," and you see immediately what he means. No single word or gesture is as important as their speech and behavior in aggregate; the *sound* of their talk, rather than any single line, conveys with devastating accuracy the vacuous and self-conscious intellectualizing that passes for insight within the white urban professional class.

Perhaps most striking, however, is the remarkable variability among May's performances, which complement the unexpected rhythms of her screenplays. As one of her earliest interviewers noted in the *New Yorker*, "[May] can arrange her features and tune her voice in so many different ways that it is impossible to say what she really looks or sounds like" (Rice 47).[37] James Morrison similarly picked up on May's exceptional versatility, noting the contrast not only with Nichols's much narrower range but also with postwar contemporaries such as Mel Brooks and Woody Allen, who "both devised distinctive comic personae" (114). May's mutability can surface even within a single performance. In the context of *Luv*, for instance, her character shifts within the span of the film from the sophisticated, self-possessed housewife struggling with ennui to someone deranged by emotion. In *A New Leaf*, May's body language manages to convey the impression that Henrietta is at once helpless and professionally accomplished; thus, May plays the character as both clumsy (tripping and dropping teacups) and blindly daring when it comes to her research (lowering herself over a cliff to retrieve plants and paddling a canoe head-on into the approaching rapids).

It is May's handling of time, however, that may be among the most unappreciated aspects of her acting style and the one that most illuminates her approach as a director. Watching May's comedic performances in *A New Leaf* or her later collaborations with Allen, it becomes clear that she uses tropes of femininity—fragility, helplessness, ditziness—to decelerate the narrative pace, forcing the slowdown, if not the full stoppage, of classic screwball comedy's breakneck rhythms. *A New Leaf*, for instance, includes the running gag that Henrietta is so uncoordinated that she requires near constant assistance, a trait that dilates and thus disrupts the default beats of a scene. In *The Heartbreak Kid*, Jeannie Berlin's Lila has a similar effect: she takes time ordering breakfast, dressing for dinner, or packing for the beach and moves with a deliberateness and lack of haste that frustrate not just her new husband but also the film's narrative pace (McElhaney). *Crisis in Six Scenes* provides a perfect vehicle for May inasmuch as it is continually willing to prioritize character work over plot, with the result that, as one reviewer noted critically, "scenes run longer than they would ordinarily; there is time for digression, to pay the doctor a visit and work in a few typical jokes about hypochondria . . . unrelated to the rest of the action" (Lloyd). As an actor, May doesn't so much play the straight man (or woman) so much as provide a different kind of comic foil, the character who refuses to be hurried, to accommodate some preordained set of narrative expectations. (That May refuses to be pressured in real life, too, was fully in evidence at her recent appearance at 92Y: despite her charge to interview friend and producer Julian Schlossberg, she purposefully dithered, deprecated her own capacities as an interlocuter, and took audience questions instead.[38])

These instances of comic stonewalling anticipate the more extreme forms of narrative dilation and digression that take place in *Mikey and Nicky* even as they reflect her own capacity, noted above, "to go on and on." That film's protracted scenes reflect a heterodox approach to scene structure in which, as Veronica Fitzpatrick writes, "scenes don't so much build and culminate as they endure or simply end." In this sense, May establishes in the rhythms of her performance some of the more eccentric narrative tendencies of her films.

Just as May's performances reflect a tendency to "take the unlikely choice," then, her direction elides anticipated beats as a mechanism for pursuing the unexpected or unexcavated truth. Writing of May's performance in *The Waverly Gallery*, its playwright, Kenneth Lonergan, described May's at times exasperatingly detailed preparations for her role: "In another actor this kind of thing would be sociopathically pretentious. In Elaine you realized you were watching, and participating in, through her dogged, persistent, perfectly civil engagement, the sinking of a foundation which was to support a spontaneity." It is a useful construction to carry into analyses of May's films, whose preparation may have appeared excessive to some but which proved to be the enabling foundation for the creation of a virtuosic if often unsettling spontaneity.

To watch May's films, in other words, is to watch cinema in which nothing has been inherited or predetermined, nothing taken for granted. Instead, the impression produced is of extreme precision, of watching the sum total of innumerable decisions, deliberately made by May, who involved herself in all aspects of her film's production and editing, and by her actors, whose performances, like her own, were often informed by extensive rehearsal. That the result of this rigorous preparation is an ambient unpredictability—a sense of not knowing from moment to moment where a scene is headed—might seem like a paradox, but it is in fact that hallmark of May's comedy, the improvisational methods she both helped to craft and would carry into her filmmaking.

A *New Leaf* and *The Heartbreak Kid*: Unromantic Comedies

> Un- is a potent invocation, a spell that doesn't make something silently disappear but instead wildly transfigures it, working a dark alchemy to make something entirely new. Un- is the sign and cipher of women's creation and revolt.
>
> —Sarah Chihaya, *The Ferrante Letters*

Elaine May's second film, *The Heartbreak Kid* (1972), begins with images of its protagonist *rushing*: first, in and out of buildings, apparently plying his trade as a sporting-goods salesman; and then, after just a few short dates, into marriage. By minute 6 of the film, Lenny Cantrow and his new bride, Lila Kolodny, are speeding down the highway in the same white car glimpsed in the opening frames, en route to a fateful honeymoon in Miami Beach.

Such extreme temporal compression represents one of the mild-to-moderate forms of estrangement that May employs both in *The*

Heartbreak Kid and in her first feature, *A New Leaf*, to subtly but unmistakably transform—or darkly "transfigure"—the romantic comedy, the genre to which both of these films at least nominally belong. May, of course, was hardly alone among 1970s directors in modifying the tradition's mainstays, or "updating the Thirties screwball comedy of remarriage for the Seventies age of the anti-hero" (Guest, "Comic Vision"). The New Hollywood period famously licensed and even rewarded certain modes of revisionism, resulting in a wave of what scholars have termed variously "radical romantic comedies" (McDonald), "nervous romances" (Neale and Krutnik), or the "transition through the counter-culture cluster" (Grindon). As I've suggested above, however, May's opportunistic approach led to more varied and subtle modes of transformation. Seen in this light, the condensation of Lenny and Lila's courtship seems designed to comment on the trope of the "whirlwind romance," with May's breathless montage and abrupt cuts ironically affirming that, yes, fools do rush in. It doesn't feel like a coincidence that *A New Leaf* also begins with a show of male heedlessness: a sequence in which its protagonist speeds down the highway in a malfunctioning sports car, only to once again stall out in the streets of Manhattan.

What makes May's comedies *un*romantic, in other words— transfigurative in the way critic Sarah Chihaya suggests—is their skepticism about the genre's principal clichés and their intimation that the pursuit of partnership is driven by desires that that are darkly perverse, if not deranged. It's true that neither of May's first two features looks especially subversive, especially compared to the "antiromances" of the decade, which tended to broadcast their transgressive credentials more frankly, whether through explicit content, experimental narrative structures, or a focus on "disaffected youth" (Deighan 99). Alongside the hip nihilism of *The Graduate* (1967), the pseudobohemianism of *Bob and Carol and Ted and Alice* (1969), or the neurotic realism of *An Unmarried Woman* (1978), May's comparably mainstream comedies, with their middle-aged or middle-American characters, would seem to qualify them as more pro- than countercultural. Her choice to feature meek or immiserated female characters might also scan as comparably regressive (as it did to feminist critics of the era), especially compared to the comparatively progressive representations of women's agency that writers like Molly Haskell discerned in classic screwball comedy. Yet such objections, which were especially directed at Lila's characterization in *The Heartbreak Kid*, overlook the fact that the humiliation of May's women is a precondition for exposing the immorality of her men. These "bad" representations, in other words, exist within the films' more complex and totalizing critiques of the marriage plot. They deliberately rather than accidentally address what J. Hoberman sees as May's central themes: "the abjectness of women and the idiocy of men" ("In *Mikey and Nicky*").

Across all three of her comedies, May's interventions become most visible at scale rather than in single tendencies or gestures and in their style as much as their substance. In my discussion of her first two films, I consider formal practices and design elements specific to each—the subtly estranging mise-en-scène of *A New Leaf* and the deliberate camera placements of *The Heartbreak Kid*—as well as those characteristic of both, namely, May's theatrical handling of space, time, and performance. While other scholars have attended to certain of these dimensions in May's filmmaking, the goal of this synthetic account is to provide a more comprehensive picture of May's transfigurative aesthetics in practice. If film studies has a robust language for documenting the visibly Brechtian tactics of the art cinema (those directors with what we might call "big" subversive energy), then May's work presents both a challenge and an opportunity to viewers in that it requires a recalibration of critical method, an attentiveness to practices that seem to originate outside of cinema, including in the realm of improvisatory performance. Close analysis reveals the many ways May's signature comes forward and the distinctive nature of her comic sensibility.

A New Leaf: The Estranged Frame

May directed her debut film, *A New Leaf*, under duress. After she wrote the screenplay, adapted from a short story by Jack Ritchie called "A Green Heart," which appeared in *Alfred Hitchcock's Mystery Magazine* in 1963, Paramount offered her the option to also star in and direct the film. The studio's motivation was hardly altruistic. Rather, it saw the chance to "exploit [May's] skills and her position in the industry because she was a first-time director and a woman" and paid her just $50,000. (By contrast, costar Walter Matthau received $375,000 for his performance [Smukler, *Liberating Hollywood* 81].) May, meanwhile, felt that directing would afford her a greater degree of creative agency than she might otherwise enjoy, even if it also ended up affording her less rather than more money. May's anecdotal accounting of her ambivalent entry into the profession, like all of her self-reporting, must be taken with a grain of salt. It's clear, after all, that she had enough interest in directing to accept the job, however reluctantly. Regardless, it was at least somewhat by accident that May—a filmmaking novice, by her own admission, who knew nothing about things such as coverage and body doubles—ended up directing her screen premiere.[39]

A New Leaf tells the story of formerly well-to-do bachelor Henry Green, who discovers at the start of the film that his fiscal irresponsibility has, to his great surprise and chagrin, left him bankrupt. Explaining to his Jeeves-like butler, Harold, that he possesses "no skills, no resources, no ambitions"—other than to be rich—he determines that the only possible course of action is to marry and then murder a rich heiress. He succeeds in his plan by wooing and wedding the kind, klutzy, and "enormously wealthy" botanist Henrietta Lowell, played by May herself. Gradually, she awakens in Henry a grudging affection, but only after he plots her death and nearly carries it off before a pang of conscience intervenes. Notably, the film as May imagined it would have been significantly darker. Her original three-hour version included a number of the plot developments—involving blackmail and several murders—present in the original story, but they were eventually cut by Paramount chief Robert Evans, who was concerned both by the film's length and by the prospect of a comic lead who commits multiple homicides. May sued Paramount, but the judge ruled in the studio's favor, and it is this shortened theatrical cut that remains the one available to audiences.

Just as important as what the studio removed from May's film, however, is what she succeeded in adding: how she gave the story's ghoulishly comic premise such striking visual expression and how her choices accrue in force and meaning across the film. Her direction is perhaps most visible in what Alexandra Heller-Nicholas calls the "overt theatricality" of *A New Leaf*, with its largely static camera, proscenium-like treatment of space, and character-driven approach, clearly indebted to May's background in theater (6). This contention is at odds with a strain of criticism that has dismissed the film's style on the grounds of amateurism. Reviewing *The Heartbreak Kid*, for instance, Pauline

Kael compared its technical proficiency favorably to May's "wobbly first movie" in that "it isn't shot in murko-color, and the framing of the action—the whole look of it—is professional" ("New Thresholds" 128). Yet I'd suggest that the noticeable unslickness of *A New Leaf*'s style only enhances the expressive force of the film's images.

May's sensibility particularly comes forward, I would argue, through her use of the frame and the film's highly curated and idiosyncratic mise-en-scène. Almost any given shot features ironic scenic elements and a distinctive approach to blocking, set, and costume design—the latter overseen by Anthea Sylbert—that collectively finesse signification. It's worth noting that costume assumes a drolly comic function within all four of May's films; one could think, for instance, of Jeannie Berlin's statement jewelry in *The Heartbreak Kid*, Ned Beatty's high-water pants in *Mikey and Nicky*, and Dustin Hoffman's kimonos and headbands in *Ishtar*. The combined rhetorical effect can be to knock viewers' inference-making off balance, a tactic that recalls May's similarly destabilizing methods in her work with Nichols. If we accept Adrian Martin's contention that mise-en-scène exists to "*sho[w]* us something; it is a means of display" (xv), then the stylized and slightly askew environs of *A New Leaf* conveys the dubious attitude with which the film seems to regard its own narrative proceedings.

The staging and framing of Henry and Henrietta's wedding presents a case in point. As a whole, the episode functions as high farce: from the opening moments, in which a young guest, Miss Heinrich, mistakes Henry's dressing room for the bathroom; to the ceremony itself, which is inaugurated by Miss Heinrich's toilet flush and features the groom being literally dragged down the aisle. More than a coherent sequence, the wedding is presented as a loosely connected series of gags, a romantic comic ritual that May strips for parts. Elements within the frame deliver supplemental critique. Following Miss Heinrich's blunder, for instance, we see Henry's butler, Harold, escort the young girl away; as they walk past the guests, the pair—wearing tails and a white dress—present as an ersatz couple whose procession away from the crowd offers a mock image of the march down the aisle.

These are the kinds of visual jokes that often show up in the edges or background of May's frame, the scenic equivalent of the throwaway lines that punctuate her screenplay. These lines are unmarked but abundant.

Figure 5. *A New Leaf*'s mock wedding march |

For instance, Henry hands his lawyer a case of unfiltered cigarettes, telling him to "smoke them in good health," while in a later scene, Henrietta's lawyer murmurs to himself as he schemes to prevent her marriage, "Who do I know who's pregnant and a good sport." None of these lines, unsurprisingly, are to be found in the original story; they are May's additions. As Melissa Anderson points out, there is a "pinpoint absurdity [to] her throwaway lines, which sometimes take a second or two to process—*did I hear that correctly?*" May's visual gags may be comparatively more marked, but they often still qualify as examples of what Kyle Stevens has dubbed "dry" as opposed to "wet" humor, the nature of which is that "it can go undetected, missed by the wrong sort of listener" ("Politics" 9). For all their self-evident, which is to say "wetter" humor, May's comedies consistently presume in their formal construction a degree of audience discernment, the likelihood of a visual double-take: Did I *see* that correctly?

May also uses the frame to offer more overt commentary, creating compositions that heighten dramatic irony and comic disjunction. On their honeymoon, for instance, while Henry sits in the foreground, researching poisons he might use to dispatch his new bride, Henrietta—in the background—examines herself in the mirror, nervously readying herself for love. May repeats the joke in a later shot, which juxtaposes Henry in extreme close-up, nose buried in a book on toxicology, with

Figure 6. May's multilayered frame |

Henrietta, who dangles off a cliff in the distance, collecting plant specimens—almost *inviting* accidental death. Behind them both, a barely visible couple paddles a canoe toward the horizon line, a detail that anticipates the couple's own disastrous canoe ride in the concluding sequence.

It's a distillation of May's visual aesthetic, a mise-en-scène that layers more obvious visual gags with darker, less marked asides. Later, for instance, having moved into his wife's house, Henry pays a visit to the greenhouse to grill the gardener about the availability of common poisons; as they speak, the two men stand positioned behind a mound of dirt resembling a freshly dug grave. Similarly, in the earlier scene when the characters first meet, Henrietta is seated in front of a fresco portraying amorous cupids, a counterpoint to the couple's own pending encounter, which could hardly be less erotic.

A New Leaf, in other words, practices something like "thick" visual description, continually providing more detail than what is narratively required. (In this sense, it preserves the original intention of farce, from the Latin *facire*, meaning "overstuffed.") One rhetorical effect of the surplus detail is to not only underscore but also at times destabilize meaning; much like the winks that the scurrilous housekeeper gives Henry, it's unclear what some of these offhanded gestures definitively "mean." Notably, May would manage something similar in *The*

Heartbreak Kid, a film in which she exercised less control over the contents of the screenplay yet successfully managed through the mise-en-scène (among other means) to inflect the story. Midway through that film, for example, Lila, the jilted wife, watches TV alone in her hotel room while waiting the return of her philandering husband, Lenny. Visible on-screen is *The Darwin Adventure* (1972), not only a less romantically auspicious choice than the one referenced in Neil Simon's screenplay—a "heated love scene" from an unnamed Clark Gable and Myrna Loy picture—but also a nod to Lenny's own "adventuring" (Shelley 72; Neil Simon 51).

Particularly suggestive in this regard is the extensive use of greenery within *A New Leaf*'s mise-en-scène. Over the course of the film, the artfully designed interiors of the first third give way to the verdant grounds of Henrietta's estate, in which every room seemingly features at least one fern, bouquet, or hanging plant. Of course, Henrietta's work as a botanist justifies the visual emphasis on plant life, but the growing dominance of green within the frame also becomes a kind of slow-burn punch line—a way of signaling that it is the seemingly hapless Henrietta, not the scheming Henry, who secretly has the upper hand. May's joke culminates in the final sequence, which unfolds in the deep green forests of the Adirondacks, in which Henry's bright red jacket marks him as the incongruous element; it's there, finally, that he will resign himself

Figure 7. Resistance through mise-en-scène |

to marriage and to the happy ending Henrietta has envisioned for them both. At scale, May seems to practice something like what, borrowing from Richard Dyer, we might call resistance through mise-en-scène—a means of communicating through scenic elements the film's allegiance with its unassuming heroine.[40]

Not all of May's additions are subtle. The introduction of Miss Heinrich, for instance, seems designed to provide a target for Henry's barely suppressed misogyny. Henry reacts to her entrance with immediate anger ("Why are you standing there, you little spy?!"), and his hostility toward this preadolescent girl is as excessive as it is revealing of his own heterosexual panic: "I will not get dressed in front of a woman, and she might as well understand that now!" he yells. Conversely, the brief fantasy sequences, which detail Henry's speculative plans for femicide, are the vestiges of studio-excised scenes whose presence would have placed the film even more squarely in the tradition of murderous marital comedies such as *Kind Hearts and Coronets* (1949) and *How to Murder Your Wife* (1965).

Blocking provides a complementary platform for May's irreverent vision. Repeatedly, May inserted minor characters in *A New Leaf*—including Henrietta's lawyer, McPherson, and members of her household staff—between the central couple, figuratively and at times literally marginalizing them within the frame. The blocking and framing of the

Figure 8. Crowding out the couple |

wedding ceremony functions similarly. May places the camera above and behind the officiant, partly obscuring the couple; behind them hovers McPherson, who harbors a crush on Henrietta and whose muffled but increasingly loud sobs threaten to drown out the sermon.

May's interventions are also evident within the soundtrack and the film's sonic as well as scenic elements. Of particular note is the symphony of tweeting birds that we hear as Henry, with comic belatedness and mock-heroic stoicism, confronts the fact of his penury; "I'm *poor*," he murmurs repeatedly to himself as he makes the rounds of his previous high-class Manhattan haunts. Punctuating the absurdism of Henry's farewell tour ("Goodbye! Goodbye!" he calls to Madison Avenue, Lutèce, and the New York Health and Racquet Club) is the false cheer of the chirping bird calls that accompany the montage. Even more potent, however, may be the voice May uses for Henrietta—soft, nasal, slightly New York accented—which provides a consistent foil to Henry's pretensions: her slow, earnest delivery, combined with the character's literalism, acts as a slow-acting solvent to his confidence scheme. If the screwball comedy has historically featured and been defined by the verbal compatibility of its leads—however poorly matched they might seem to be in terms of circumstance or temperament—May's insistence on the extreme *misalignment* of her couple's expressive pace feels like one of the film's most original gestures (Kozloff 174).[41] It is a dimension that makes the studio's decision to dub May's voice at several points in the film—including its closing minutes—all the more egregious.

Essential Shtick

May makes room for seemingly additive elements not just within the frame but also within the film's narrative economy. Put another way, *A New Leaf*—with its static two-shots, proscenium-like setups, and commitment to let scenes play—has a pace and set of dialogue-driven priorities that can feel more indebted to theater. One early example is a protracted, recursive exchange between Henry and his lawyer, whom May has aptly named Beckett, an apparent nod to the scene's exhausting, escalating absurdism, as Henry continually fails to grasp the basic fact of his bankruptcy. "Come to the point, Beckett!" Henry demands nonsensically as Beckett calmly rejoins, for the umpteenth time, "The point, Mr. Graham, is that you don't have any money."

Not surprisingly, this proliferation of the narratively nonessential was received by some at the studio as a liability. During production, for instance, one of the Paramount executives, Peter Bart, complained about the film's excesses; as Maya Montañez Smukler reports, he "voiced his concerns about *A New Leaf*'s screenplay to Robert Evans. Bart was critical of what he saw as a disjointed story with moments of long-winded and unnecessary dialogue" (*Liberating Hollywood* 82). But even more interesting may be the subsequent comment in his internal memo: "What we have here are two movies, not one. The first is comedy-satire. The second is bald farce. The first has characterizations. The second has only shtick. I like the first. I dislike the second" (qtd. on 82). Bart's invocation of shtick is particularly telling. It is the kind of Yiddishism that recurs in May's work, one that, in *Ishtar*, is conflated with the idea of the gimmick. ("You got no shtick. You got no gimmicks!") As Sianne Ngai argues, the term *gimmick* is often used as a casual pejorative to communicate the suspicion that something is at once contrived and insubstantial, working too hard and not hard enough. Yet the film's seemingly superfluous elements serve a rhetorically essential function, highlighting the sheer artifice—the gimmickry—of social convention. What is courtship, in other words, *but* shtick?

At the same time, the film's structure serves to accommodate the performance-driven nature of May's work—to give herself and her fellow actors time and space. In this sense, *A New Leaf* reflects a kind of ethos of accommodation whereby elements need not serve a single narrative telos to be included in the film or within the frame. *A New Leaf*'s embrace of seemingly ancillary visual and verbal elements may actually bear less family resemblance to the tradition of American screwball comedies than to the darker and more socially critical strains of the *commedia all'italiana*.[42] For instance, Peter Bondanella cites director Mario Monicelli's observation that Italian comic films of this period "united laughter with a sense of desperation" (181), and something analogous might said of May's early comedies. In *Divorce Italian Style* (1961), for instance, Marcello Mastroianni plays a more charming but no less amoral iteration of Walter Matthau's murderous husband. His motivation is not money but rather, like Lenny in *The Heartbreak Kid*, erotic obsession with another, unavailable woman. But the film shares with May's both an amused detachment from its male protagonist and a commitment to showcasing—in the form of interpolated fantasy sequences—his most violent desires.

That *A New Leaf*, like *The Heartbreak Kid*, was ultimately a success with audiences and critics suggests that the film's stylistic eccentricities and emphasis on performance over expeditious progression were far from disqualifying. Working from the bare template of Ritchie's story and stymied by studio interference, May nonetheless managed to create in *A New Leaf* not only a qualified hit but also one of cinema's most hilarious rebuttals to the foundational "moves" of romantic comedy (Grindon 8–12). Henry and Henrietta don't "meet cute"; their encounter is contrived and lacks sexual chemistry. Their "fun together" is for Henry largely tortuous, while the climactic "epiphany" leads not to the couple's joyous reconstitution but to affectionate resignation. And when, on their honeymoon night, the two characters approach each other, the encounter is centered around Henrietta's recalcitrant "Grecian-style" nightgown, with an emphasis not on trying to remove the garment but on better covering her with it. "You have your head through the armhole," Henry repeats mechanically. "Where is your head hole?"

It's a brilliant send-up of wedding night jitters and conjugal fumbling, with the bride and groom working, with great assiduousness, to *find the right hole*. Even as the film nods to the consummation of marriage, then,

Figure 9. Nightgown shtick: looking for the right hole

May's focus as always is on the absurd, basically arbitrary mechanics of coupling and the reversal of any clichés that would lead audiences to imagine otherwise.

The Heartbreak Kid: Assimilation and Distance

If May's second feature, *The Heartbreak Kid*, is more realist in its presentation of the central relationship—less overtly theatrical, less reliant on farce—it also makes use of a different set of disillusioning tactics. Most significant may be the forms of distance, literal and figurative, that May inserts between the viewer and the film's protagonist, Lenny Cantrow, a Jewish sporting goods salesman from New York who jilts his new bride, Lila, after falling for lithe shiksa coed Kelly during his and Lila's honeymoon in Miami. Lenny is in nearly every frame of the film yet is hardly ever seen in close-up. (Indeed, it's a notable feature of May's filmmaking that her characters are infrequently alone; they almost always appear in pairs or as part of a group.) Instead, May regularly portrays Lenny in medium or long shots. The impression produced is of looking at the protagonist rather than with him. Put another way, May's version of *The Heartbreak Kid* may be focused on Lenny, but it is only weakly focalized through him, a distinction that remains central to understanding how May handles her male characters: ironically, at some distance.

It is worth emphasizing how markedly this approach differs from the one adopted by Neil Simon's screenplay, itself loosely based on Bruce Jay Friedman's short story "A Change of Plan," originally published in *Esquire* in 1966. Simon's first draft, from August 1971, prescribes numerous close-ups, and Simon regularly includes slug lines and stage directions designed to center Lenny's viewpoint ("the camera moves in on Lenny's face," "we are in tight on his face," "very close, full face," etc.). For the most part, however, these instructions don't appear to have been observed by May, who seems to have taken a latitude with camerawork—as well as with casting and performance—that she was technically prohibited from taking with Simon's language, according to the terms of his contract.

A closer review of Simon's original screenplay—now available among his archived papers—suggests that May might have deviated even more substantially from the script than has been recognized. Below, I catalog some of the major changes May appears to have introduced into the film, including a new introductory sequence and a radically different conclusion. These are in addition to the separate changes and cuts requested by Palomar pictures producer Ed Scherick in a memo dated January 1972. While Simon's papers do include some edited scenes in response to Palomar's suggestions, it is clear that May, by Simon's admission, did her own significant rewrites. Asked about whether May attempted "some end runs around" the contractual stipulation—that "nothing could be rewritten without [his] approval"—Simon confirmed that "she did, and I could have really screamed about it; but some of the changes I liked. Some of them I *didn't* like, but it's not worth it to go through what she herself did [on *A New Leaf*]. . . . I was for the most part very happy with *Heartbreak Kid*, so I said OK. So I lost a few battles here and there" (qtd. in Brady 329–30). Among the changes he didn't like was May's ending; as Simon put it, "I thought the ending of the picture that I wrote was infinitely better than what Elaine had," a point he would repeatedly emphasize: "I thought my ending was better. They shot it. They filmed it and never showed it to anybody. . . . I'm not furious at Elaine for wanting to try it, because she did it both ways; but it was the obligation of the producer . . . to screen it and see how others feel about it" (330). Significantly, this is one of the only interviews in which Simon discussed the film or its adaptation in much detail—a sign, some suggest, of his frustration with May's methods. Despite Simon's own contention that he "was there [on set] every day, rewriting," Grodin and others have reported that he was in fact barely present during production (Bryer and Siegel 63).

Even putting aside for the moment those major plot revisions, it is clear that May significantly reshaped the script's characterization of Lenny in large part through her approach to camera placement. Simon's screenplay is openly sympathetic to Lenny, using stage directions to align audiences literally and figuratively with his point of view: "The camera moves in on Lenny's face. There is trouble here" (10), "The camera moves in closer and closer to LENNY'S eyes until they fill the screen with his desperation" (15), "The camera closes in on him. Can a man look both ecstatic and worried?" (54). The script is proportionally hostile to Lila, making her unambiguously grotesque and amplifying the character's cloying, infantile behaviors. For instance, in Simon's script,

Lila complains that she needs to "go pee pee" not once as in May's film, but three times; she forgets to flush the toilet, and later she gets stuck in the bathroom, yelling to Lenny: "I'll be down in about 10 minutes. I'm having a little doopy trouble" (21). In May's film there's a scene in which Lila savors a candy bar after sex, trying to force it on Lenny ("Don't put a Milky Way in someone's mouth when they don't want it"), a joke that is both less developed in Simon's screenplay and repeated several times. Lila's sunburn—a vehicle for physical comedy in the film that leads to Jeannie Berlin's overzealous application of soothing cream—is in Simon's screenplay an opportunity for derisive comments about her appearance and for casual racism as well as sexism. As Simon writes of the character, "Her eyes are two little slits peeking out through two mountains of inflated flesh. SHE looks like a Chinese heavyweight who has just decisively lost a title match" (36). It is possible, of course, that Simon was the one to recalibrate the script's treatment of its respective characters and that a final, unknown version qualified its contempt for Lila. But given where the script started, it seems fair to speculate that May played a major role in the redistribution of narrative empathy, as did Berlin, who has emphasized the efforts she took to humanize Lila: "You see, I didn't want to make that girl stupid. It would have been so easy to do Lila stupid. I don't think Lila was stupid. I think every single thing she did was justified to her" (qtd. in Gruen).

The distinctness of May's approach to the film's main characters becomes evident when juxtaposed not just with Simon's script but also with Mike Nichols's direction in *The Graduate*, a film to which *The Heartbreak Kid* has been frequently compared.[43] From the opening moments, Nichols encourages the viewer's identification with the film's protagonist. *The Graduate* opens with a tight close-up on Benjamin, played by Dustin Hoffman, before a reverse zoom situates him among his fellow plane passengers; the camera remains fixed on him, holding a several-minutes-long profile shot, as he glides through LAX on a moving walkway. The remainder of the film does little to dispel this proximity to the character's perspective. By contrast, Lenny is first glimpsed in a medium-long shot emerging from a car, as if accidentally caught on a closed-circuit camera.

When viewers do see Lenny's face, it's revealed through his reflection as he rehearses pick-up lines in the mirror. ("Hi," he murmurs to his

Figure 10. *The Heartbreak Kid*: keeping Lenny at
a distance

image, putting a pipe between his teeth.) Meanwhile, the theme for
this opening sequence—a catchy tune that sounds like a commercial
jingle—produces a sense of false cheer that casts a veneer of irony over
the proceedings; this is a character, we sense, who would publicly ascribe
to the kind of generic platitudes being sold in this song: "You'll be alright!
/ You're going far!" (The lyrics were written by May's former husband,
composer Sheldon Harnick.) By contrast, *The Graduate*'s solemn Simon
and Garfunkel track, "The Sound of Silence," cues a very different set
of inferences, promoting the view of a character at least aspiring to
seriousness and substance, in distinction to "people hearing without
listening." If Nichols imagines a protagonist at least hypothetically
opposed to prevailing middle-class values—a world of "plastics"—May's
protagonist is a product and promulgator of such values, a case study in
false consciousness, and an enthusiastic participant in his own ethnic
assimilation.

The sense of amused detachment that informs the film's editing,
sound cues, and camerawork has not gone unnoticed in writing about
the film. Ethan Warren, for one, highlights May's "observational style"
in *The Heartbreak Kid* and nicely captures the rhetorical effect of this
approach: "Rather than centralizing the characters' experience of the
story, she prizes the audience's subjective experience of the characters—
when Lenny and Lila share their first dance, they're shot from across the

room, leaving their conversation inaudible." Along similar lines, Mitchell Cohen noted in a contemporary review of the film a further implication of this observational method: "She lets us believe that she is guileless, totally distanced from the humor in the situation. In the role of innocent participant rather than sophisticated commentator, she allows humor to evolve where Simon's dissolves." McElhaney, similarly, understands May's "dispassionate" approach as central to her films' humor.[44]

In fact, May's gaze in *The Heartbreak Kid* is only seemingly dispassionate, her apparent noninterventionism a canny pose, permitting her to *seem* to "present without comment"—to offer this footage of Lenny for our consideration and judgment. If some feminist critics initially construed Lenny as the subject of the gaze, it seems inarguable that he is chiefly its object.[45] One brief example: Early in the film, Lenny attempts to impress Kelly, whom he has just met on the beach. Surprised by the sudden appearance of Lila, Lenny leaps up from the sand to rejoin his wife. Trying to play it cool, he tosses his sandals breezily into the air—but then fails to catch them. Scrambling to recover, he bundles his belongings into his towel, which he then slings, hobo pack style, over his shoulder and half stumbles, half skips off the beach. May shoots this highly entertaining bit of slapstick from a comfortable remove, suggesting that this little display of male vanity is primarily for the viewer's benefit.

More generally, within the couple's Miami hotel room, May consistently positions the camera across from the door, on Lila's side of the bed, to provide the better vantage from which to observe Lenny's frenzied comings and goings. As viewers, we are almost always on Lila's "side," literally, and, like her, we are witness to Lenny's increasingly outlandish lies. Within the relatively tight space of their room, May creates a clear proscenium, a stage for Grodin to enact a governing principle in May's work: that "the male protagonist . . . is fundamentally a *schmuck*" (McElhaney). Thus, when Lenny returns after flirting with Kelly at the downstairs bar, the rapid reverse zoom as he reenters the room seems designed to spotlight his guilt, freezing him like a perpetrator caught midcrime.

Grodin's performance here is definitive. As Lenny doubles down on his lies, Grodin quickens the pace of his line readings even as he varies their rhythm and volume, inserting unexpected pauses and generally

Figure 11. On Lila's side |

imbuing the character with a volatility James Naremore sees as the
particular legacy of Nichols and May, who helped popularize an approach
that links "Stanislavskian techniques . . . to an absurdist mode" (281).
As noted above, he describes the resulting performance style as "less
presentational, less clearly enunciated . . . more given to free-associated
monologues . . . and apparently extemporaneous outbursts of emotion"
(282). If Grodin's style is less presentational, however, camera placement
continually establishes the character's behavior as a performance, with
Lila as its incredulous audience. The growing disparity between the placid
straight-woman and the increasingly agitated man is a staple of Nichols
and May's routines, such as "Telephone Company Information Operators"
and "$65 Funeral." Significantly, this setup also inverts the more familiar
screwball formula—exemplified by *My Man Godfrey* (1936), *Bringing
Up Baby* (1938), or *Ball of Fire* (1941)—in which it is the woman's unruly
antics that destabilize and provoke the more stolid and steady man.

As they did in *A New Leaf*, May's blocking and framing heighten
the sense of detachment from Lenny's point of view. The presence
of dorsal as opposed to frontal shots is particularly revealing. While
dorsality has been used to more emphatic, alienating effect in European
art cinema—or, in Brandon Colvin's words, to promote "compositional
defamiliarization" and deny "clear psychological/emotional access to
character" (191)—May seems to deploy it playfully in order to obviate
narrative cliché. These effects are particularly evident in the two wedding

Figures 12–13. Withholding frontal shots |

sequences that bookend *The Heartbreak Kid*. In both cases, the bride's procession down the aisle—a common and heavily freighted image in popular culture—is shown only from behind, the anticipated sight of the woman in a white dress conspicuously withheld. During the first ceremony, May repeatedly cuts away from key moments; during the second, she compromises the couple's centrality by panning left, away from the groom and toward the lunky local also-rans who had previously competed for Kelly's affections.

At other points, May's staging heightens Lenny's distance not just from the viewers but also from the world he is most intensely eager to join. *The Heartbreak Kid*, much like *Ishtar*, frequently invites us to see the main characters through the eyes of "minor" ones. During one extended sequence, a single set-up in which Lenny sits down with Kelly's father—a buttoned-up midwestern patriarch who is clearly repulsed by his daughter's Jewish suitor—May positions Grodin and the actor Eddie Albert in the extreme foreground on opposite sides of the frame, with Kelly and her mother between and behind them. Though the two women are slightly out of focus, they are sufficiently *in* focus for their reactions to the men's exchange to be visible. While Lenny attempts to "lay his cards on the table," undeterred by Mr. Corcoran's obvious hostility and simmering anti-Semitism, Cybill Shepherd as Kelly smirks in the background, amused by this spectacle of male competition.

Later, Shepherd does some similar mugging at the dinner table as Grodin delivers a grandiose and (it turns out) unoriginal speech about the "honesty" of the food being served: "There's no lying in the beef, there's no insincerity in these potatoes. There's no deceit in that cauliflower!" Even as Shepherd's character is supposedly enamored of Lenny, Shepherd's *performance* hints at the dubiousness of that prospect. When Kelly remarks for her parents' benefit on Lenny's "positivity" ("Isn't he *positive*, Mama?" she asks, a line that refers back to her earlier comment to Lenny, "You're so *positive* about everything"),

Figure 14. Smirking at the men |

the layers of performance within the scene, alongside Shepherd's arch line reading, lend an ironic edge to her praise. Kelly's expression of faith in manly "positivity," after all, follows on the heels of a speech her father deems "the biggest crock of horseshit [he has] ever heard in his life." Similarly, in *A New Leaf*, Henrietta celebrates Henry's confidence ("Oh, you're so *positive!*") only minutes after his car has broken down—a juxtaposition that highlights, if only for viewers, the distance between the male characters' aspirations and their real-life acumen.

If May's direction of *The Heartbreak Kid* often seems maximized for the exposure of masculine pretense, that's not to say it doesn't have other targets. In this same dinner sequence, for instance, shot from Kelly's father's point of view highlights Lenny's status as a Jewish outlier within the homogeneously white Protestant world of the snowy Midwest. As McElhaney notes, "The dark-haired Lenny becomes the incongruous point of contrast in this image, otherwise dominated by blonde and silver-haired Gentiles." This image of failed assimilation anticipates the more broadly comic scene of Jewish alienation in *Annie Hall* (1977), in which Alvy Singer sits down to a holiday dinner with the Hall clan, only to flash to an image of himself dressed in Orthodox garb at this table of unsmiling WASPs. In May's film, the primary spectacle may be male self-deceit, but a close second is the barely contained anti-Semitism directed toward Lenny, the ethnic interloper into this Protestant idyll.

Figure 15. Lenny: ethnic interloper I

Painfully Funny: May's Discomfort-Dealing Comedy

The more intensely Lenny's behavior transmutes into a performance—the more fevered the pretense—the greater the comedy and, eventually, the tragedy as we watch the symbolic death of Lenny's salesman, hocking himself to middle America. There is something almost poignant about his frenzied efforts at assimilation, the desperation behind Lenny's antic pursuit of happiness and "positivity." To a greater degree than May's other films—but like her early play *Adaptation*—*The Heartbreak Kid* is about the automated nature of social performance. The genius of May's approach is her entirely *un*-Simon-like refusal to spoon-feed us ideas; instead, she merely pulls back the curtain, exposing the mechanics of middle-class striving, whose pointlessness she reveals in the final shot of Lenny, utterly alone, seemingly stunned. Should we laugh? Cry? Both?

Indeed, one of the most indelible sequences in *The Heartbreak Kid* elicits discomfort as much as laughter. The occasion is a long-deferred lobster dinner. The audience knows, though Lila does not, that Lenny plans to break up with her over dessert. When the scene starts, Lila is smiling and cracking lobster claws, but the comic energy dissipates over the next twelve minutes as Lenny begins, in the most circuitous way possible, to disentangle himself from their marriage. After some digressive chitchat—the kitchen has run out of what Lenny calls the "yummy yummy pecan pie"—and pedantic speech-making about the value of "life!" Lila finally thinks she has understood her husband's confession. "Oh, Lenny, you're dying!" she sobs, collapsing in his arms as he immediately rejoins, "I'm not dying! Who said anything about dying? I want out of the marriage!" May immediately cuts from the couple to reaction shots of nearby patrons, then back to Lila, nauseated and nearly catatonic from shock. She tries, repeatedly, to excuse herself to the bathroom ("I'm going to throw up"), while Lenny pulls her back to the table, his prattle about pie and generous divorce settlements sounding more deranged by the minute.

It is at once the film's most affecting and most estranging sequence. The montage of disapproving glances cast in Lenny's direction has a mildly distancing effect, even as the naturalism of Berlin's performance keeps events grounded in real emotion. In this sense, May's approach feels not unlike the one Rainer Werner Fassbinder employed in his Sirk-inspired films, which modified a popular American genre to make viewers "feel *and* think" (qtd. in Sparrow).[46] In particular, this

Figure 16. Comedy of discomfort |

scene recalls one in *Ali: Fear Eats the Soul* (1974)—released two years after *The Heartbreak Kid*—in which another emotionally heightened conversation between a couple at a restaurant is intercut with shots of the café's staff, who are leveling judgmental stares at the couple's table. In Fassbinder's film, the onlookers comprise a hostile tableau; in May's, the much briefer reaction shots provide a less totalizing form of defamiliarization. Yet their insertion nonetheless exerts a similar effect, creating space to reflect not on the bigotry of the onlookers, as in Fassbinder's film, but on the cruelties that can subtend a marriage.

Figure 17. Time to react |

The insertion of these peripheral reactions is just one way May breaks up and slows down the proceedings. She also adjusts the pace by building in, or having the actors build in, pauses in the dialogue's delivery. As Ethan Warren has observed, such beats are central to May's adaptation of Simon's work, which she "suffuses . . . with silences—languid ones with no comic stopwatch running." Or in this case, excruciating ones that invite viewers to find this scene *not* funny, or not *only* funny.

It is worth noting, by way of providing context for May's creative interventions, just how substantially her approach to Neil Simon's material differed from that of contemporary directors in the 1970s. Both Herbert Ross's *California Suite* (1978) and Arthur Hiller's *The Out-of-Towners* (1970) are illustrative in this regard: slaves to the rhythms of Simon's screenplays, they march the actors through the lines at a rapid and occasionally joyless clip. (A notable exception: the episode in *California Suite* in which May appears with Walter Matthau.) In *The Heartbreak Kid*, by contrast, the actors' delivery creates the impression of language being really spoken. Even Pauline Kael, no fan of Simon's, notes admiringly that in May's hands "the dialogue sounds natural and unforced" ("New Thresholds" 126). As Cybill Shepherd recalls, May directed them toward this end, telling her actors, "When you deliver a line, say it as if you expect the other character to be hearing you, getting it" (110). The sense of looseness, then, was both utterly intentional and, as mentioned above, absolutely unnerving to Simon during his early visits to the set: "Simon was appalled to find May directing her actors to sing in the car when he hadn't written singing into the script" (Warren). The result was that "they struck an uneasy deal: each scene would be filmed twice, once with full deference to the script and once with the space for discovery. It wasn't long, however, before Simon gave up and left *The Heartbreak Kid* in Elaine May's hands. In Simon's own memoirs, neither May nor the film merit[s] more than a passing mention" (Warren). Grodin has confirmed how discomfited Simon was by May's improvisational approach, though as Cybill Shepherd notes, "she didn't call it that": "She spoke about the exploration of subtext, the meaning beneath the lines" (110). But it is precisely May's subordination of Simon's script to her actors' explorations that makes the film not just the more successful adaptation but also, frankly, the funnier film. May is endlessly inventive in her delay tactics, playing with time much as she played with space in *A New Leaf*. Having the actors sing, chew gum, and, in Jeannie Berlin's case, dress (and, at one point, undress) with deliberate slowness are all mechanisms for finding room within Simon's screenplay. If a frantic pace is associated with Lenny throughout the film—as implied by the opening anecdote and by Lila's explicit question, "Where are you rushing to?"—May continually sides with Lila in slowing down.

Recalibrating the pace in this way is just one of the ways May modifies Simon's script and—as in her adaptation of Jack Ritchie's story—brings her own, edgier sensibility forward. Among her most important changes was to make the character of Lila Jewish, as she was not in Simon's screenplay, a modification that serves a characterizing function and an ideological one, allowing the film to address cultural as well as sexual politics (McElhaney).[47] But a closer look at Simon's original draft suggests that May played a more active role in shaping this "work-for-hire" project than has traditionally been assumed (Warren).

Indeed, reading Simon's original screenplay reveals how much more heavy-handed the film might have been had May not exercised the influence she evidently did and if Ed Scherick had not required cuts in several scenes for cost-saving purposes. The philosophy behind what Warren calls Simon's "blunt force script" seems to be, Why make the joke once when you can make it multiple times? Pauline Kael was particularly devastating on the subject of Simon's screenplays and "pandering, hard-core humor," noting cheekily that "at the movies, *who* says a line is very important, but with Neil Simon's vaudeville snappers what matters is that they come on schedule." If Kael's criticism of Simon is that his "cracking, whacking style is always telling you that things are funnier than you see them to be," by contrast, she notes approvingly, "Elaine May underplays her hand" ("New Thresholds" 127, 128).

Most significant and surprising is May's substitution of Simon's original ending with one of her own devising. In the original, 1971 screenplay, Lenny and Kelly depart on a Hollywood cruise. This time around it is Lenny who is quickly incapacitated—by seasickness, just as Lila was by sunburn—leaving Kelly to fall into an apparent dalliance with a shipmate; we end with the characters poised to reprise the initial setup in a different key. (Something not dissimilar occurs in Friedman's story, in which Lenny falls for Kelly's mother.) It is a rather uninspired

Figure 18. Alone and adrift |

ending that bears little resemblance to the quietly devastating one we see on-screen. The film's conclusion finds Lenny at his second wedding reception, making fatuous small talk, avoiding his new wife, and clearly already at loose ends. He retreats to a couch, where he attempts to chat up two nearby children, but is left alone when, after suffering politely through Lenny's spiel, they excuse themselves. As May holds the shot, Lenny begins humming "Close to You," the song he and Lila danced to at their wedding—a gesture that seems to reflect not so much true nostalgia as a kind of dazed regression.

With this image of Lenny adrift in his new and alienating WASP environs, May not only throws into doubt the viability of this particular couple, in the manner of *The Graduate*'s concluding two-shot of Benjamin and Katherine, sitting side by side in stunned silence. Instead, *The Heartbreak Kid* prompts us to question the feasibility of *any* couple and whether the drive toward coupledom doesn't itself qualify as a kind of pathology, if not a punch line.

Considered cumulatively, May's ironizing strategies raise questions about the status of both *A New Leaf* and *The Heartbreak Kid* as either romantic or comedies. Scholars have previously qualified the films' classification, with Warren, for instance, dubbing them "demented romances" and Elise Moore framing them as the first two entries in May's "sociopath trilogy." Their comedy credentials have been similarly qualified: Samm Deighan describes *A New Leaf* as an example of "screwball black comedy," and J. Hoberman, in a retrospective of May's career, dubs the film a "devastating feminist psychodrama concealed as an amiable dark comedy" ("May Days"). For Melissa Anderson, *The Heartbreak Kid* is "a deft comedy of humiliation" that spotlights the "derangements of coupledom" that recur in May's cinema. And if both films incite laughter—one of two generally agreed upon requirements for comedy—neither could be said to really fulfill the criterion of the happy ending, with *The Heartbreak Kid*'s bleak finish making *The Graduate*'s conclusion look almost measured by comparison.

What distinguishes May's comedies, in short, is their willingness to treat the basic premises of the genre with irreverence that tilts toward cynicism. Even at their most flippant, the screwball comedies of the 1930s continued to take the pursuit of love seriously, as something worth the histrionics, the antagonism, the multiplying obstacles. Similarly, even the grimmest of the 1970s "antiromances"—those focused on "couples who are miserable, destructive, or cruel to each other"—were, in dwelling on romance in its fallen state, residually affirmative of it as a vanishing ideal (Deighan 99). Perhaps the clearest forebear of May's work in Hollywood cinema may be located in the delightfully cutting comedies of Ernst Lubitsch, in which, as A. O. Scott has noted, "cynicism and romance are as firmly entwined as embracing lovers." May's cynicism, however, is less adulterated, and her films are more fully committed to the idea that marriage, far from a desideratum, is at best a detente: something to be suffered or just survived (given that *A New Leaf* puts the experience of marriage and murder into continued proximity). If one constant of romantic comedy, even in its more "radical" and postclassical mode, has been to uphold coupledom as a central project of adult lives— something to be actively pursued, if increasingly according to the terms set by sexually liberated women and queer protagonists—May's first two comedies took the radical step of presenting this outcome as at least potentially tragic.

Mikey and Nicky: Digression and Masculine Dysfunction

According to one well-known anecdote about May's third film, *Mikey and Nicky* (1976), there came a moment during production when its two leads, Peter Falk and John Cassavetes, wandered out of the frame while the camera was rolling (Blum 42). After several minutes, the camera operator yelled "Cut!" to May's apparent consternation. When the cameraman tried to justify his decision by noting that the actors had left the scene, May is said to have responded, "Yes . . . but they might come back."

This story first appeared in David Blum's profile cum exposé of *Ishtar* (1987), where it was furnished as proof of May's reckless indifference to practicalities. From today's standpoint, however, this account of May's on-set behavior lands differently. On the one hand, it underscores the degree to which the reception of May's final two films has been mediated by unfriendly press coverage, which, in its reliance on hearsay and secondhand information, has often casually blended the factual and apocryphal. In the midst of recounting this and other allegedly incriminating episodes, for instance, Blum mentions that *Mikey and Nicky* "had been largely improvised" (42). In fact, the film's dialogue was fully scripted, and the impression of spontaneity was the result of both ad-libbing during the rehearsal process and scrupulous preparation on May's part.[48]

But when considered from another angle and retold by a more reliable narrator, this anecdote serves a more positive function, illuminating the distinctive method behind May's alleged madness. This story, as shared by producer Michael Hausman during an interview with cinematographer Victor Kemper, confirms May's commitment to exploration and her tolerance for digression, qualities she had prioritized from her earliest collaborations with Nichols and cultivated during the rehearsal process in her previous films. The story also reveals that these practices were strategic, a reflection of her belief that, as *Mikey and Nicky* actor Carol Grace put it, "something extraordinary will happen if you wait long enough" (243). For May, the long take was a mechanism designed not just to capture but also actually to catalyze a degree of narrative volatility that, in turn, conveyed a central truth about the film's subjects. It's not incidental, in other words, that over the course of *Mikey and Nicky* its main characters continually swerve, scuttle plans, reverse course, or leave the frame, only to "come back," leading some spectators to conclude that the film is simply "too erratic for its own good" (Carr 125). The film's narrative structure doesn't just test viewers' tolerance for the "incoherence" associated with New Hollywood storytelling or the psychological realism popularized by Method acting, though it does both, forcing audiences into protracted alignment with profoundly dysfunctional characters. (As the movie's tagline read, "You don't have to like 'em.")[49] In the process, May's digressive film also presents a counterpoint to the portraits of damaged but charismatic masculinity offered by much auteurist cinema of the 1970s. In *Mikey and Nicky*, even more so than in May's previous films, American masculinity isn't a coherent narrative so much as a series of sidebars, reversals, and false starts.

In this light, many of the most infamous aspects of May's direction—her insistence on shooting with several cameras and on doing multiple long takes of each scene, resulting in 1.4 million feet of film—emerge as expressions of her practice rather than as evidence of her shortcomings. That's not to say there aren't drawbacks to this approach; even her closest collaborators, for instance, have admitted that the rigors and particularities of her process can prove exhausting.[50] But it's also true that whatever difficulties May's artistic commitments entailed were exacerbated by technological constraints. As Matt Carlin has pointed out, May suffered from having been "born too far ahead of the equipment required for her success": "Celluloid had a price that made Elaine May seem much more extravagant that she would seem now, shooting on the RED." May's eccentricities, in other words, would have been less noticeable—and likely less objectionable—had she had access to digital tools that would have allowed her to more easily realize her ambitions. By training the cameras so relentlessly on her characters' movements, observing the minutiae of their behavior from multiple angles and over multiple hours, May effectively gives her main characters, these two low-level hoods, the narrative rope to hang themselves with. *Mikey and Nicky*'s idiosyncratic shape thus becomes central to the delivery of its message, the formal expression of what Travis Woods has called a "corrosion-crusted portrait of terrified, putrefactive masculinity."

With *Mikey and Nicky*, then, May shifted the target of her critique from heterosexual romance to homosocial bromance and to the aggressions perpetrated in the name of another kind of coupledom. Instrumental to May's portrait of masculinity under duress is its manipulation of narrative as well as generic codes and its embrace of a more experimental visual idiom. Joe McElhaney, for one, notes the contrast between "the comparatively conventional framing and decoupage of the single-camera technique of *The Heartbreak Kid*" and "the multiple camera technique of *Mikey and Nicky*," which "gives an impression of a seemingly infinite number of set-ups." Commentators have rightly noted correspondences with the work of John Cassavetes, who costars in the film as the titular Nicky and who was similarly committed to an antiexpositional style.[51] But there has also been an unfortunate tendency to mischaracterize May's approach as a retread or pastiche of Cassavetes, one that fails to recognize the expressive purposes to which these elements are being put.[52] Of particular note is May's insistence on grounding her male protagonists' behavior in the realm of the consequential and social. It is more accurate to say that May thoughtfully adapts rather than slavishly adopts elements of Cassavetes's style with the goal of documenting *men* under the influence, as well as the impact of their behavior on the people—specifically, the women—around them.[53]

Understanding May's method as an expressive tactic not only helps to disambiguate her approach from Cassavetes, with whose work *Mikey and Nicky* has too uncritically been conflated, but also allows for appreciation of May's own auteurist practice as distinct from—and even oppositional to—that of other contemporaries. Kyle Stevens, for one, goes so far as to suggest that in *Mikey and Nicky* "May is commenting on the arguable machismo of Cassavetes' style, a machismo which is also evident in the general effects that global New Wave cinema had on American film style" ("Elaine May" 200). The fact that *Mikey and Nicky* starts where a contemporaneous film such as *The Conversation* (1974) ends—with a closed-room display of paranoia and self-destruction—suggests that May is not only wise to the depictions of masculine dysfunction in New Hollywood but also clear-eyed about their excesses and blind spots. Similarly suggestive is that one of the first shots of the film is a close-up of Nicky clutching a pistol defensively at crotch level. If *Mikey and Nicky* has been misconstrued as a product of happenstance or a showcase for her actors' improvisations, such characterizations obscure both May's artistry and her fiercely disciplined focus on the real-time dissolution of her subjects, as well as the reverberating effects of their violence.

Recovering the design undergirding the film's apparent artlessness finally allows audiences to ask new questions and to refine prevailing accounts of *Mikey and Nicky*'s creation as well as its postproduction fate. What becomes possible when we analyze the film as a product of May's artistry rather than her eccentricities? If we use studio opposition rather than individual failure as a heuristic for considering the film's final shape, critical reception, and commercial performance? If critics rewrote the story of *Mikey and Nicky*'s production not in terms of May's perfectionism but rather in terms of her precision?

Mikey and Nicky's Perverse Frequencies

At the simplest level, *Mikey and Nicky* tells the story of two small-time Philadelphia hoods, longtime friends whose intimacy is colored by a lifetime of resentments as well as deep-seated affection. The action unfolds over the course of one night as Nicky, convinced that he is the target of a mob hit, summons Mikey to the seedy hotel where Nicky is hiding out, hoping to pressure his old friend to help him flee town. As the two set off on an erratic tour of the city, the film reveals not only that Nicky's paranoia is justified but also that Mikey himself is in on the plan and actively conspiring with the bumbling hit man, Walter Kinney (played by Ned Beatty), dispatched by their boss, Dave Resnick, to kill Nicky before the night is out.

To the extent that *Mikey and Nicky* is a gangster film, however, it is also a film that voids all glamor from the genre.[54] If Francis Ford Coppola's first two installations in *The Godfather* trilogy (1972, 1974) helped consolidate both the cultural mystique and tragic romance of organized crime, *Mikey and Nicky* is closer to an antithesis—a vision of the mob stripped of any appeal, populated only by hot-headed Sonnys and ineffectual, resentful Fredos. In production at the same time as *Mean Streets* (1973), as J. Hoberman points out, May's "exhilarating feel-bad movie" is, I would argue, ultimately *more* disturbing than Scorsese's, thanks to the chilling matter-of-factness with which it documents the characters' misogyny, racism, and narcissism ("In *Mikey and Nicky*").

Mikey and Nicky's reinterpretation of the buddy film is similarly prosaic. Many of the decade's best-known examples of the genre—*Easy Rider* (1969), *Midnight Cowboy* (1969), *The Last Detail* (1973)—are populated by quixotic dreamers, but the short-sighted, hard-nosed subjects of May's film are another species, less real buddies than frenemies whose machinations are unredeemed by any ideal beyond their own survival. Even Molly Haskell's overwhelmingly negative review of the film concedes that with *Mikey and Nicky* May has "perhaps, unwittingly . . . planted the kiss of death on the buddy myth, at least for a while" ("Long Day's Journey" 37). In contrast to her earlier comedies, in which May's signature flourishes were most visible at the level of mise-en-scène, performance, and, in *A New Leaf*, dialogue, *Mikey and Nicky* embraces conspicuously experimental tactics, undermining expected forms of character development and withholding recognizable narrative beats. It is not only through the film's unflattering portrayals of its subjects, then, but in its unpredictable structure that May's vision reveals itself.

A case in point is the film's use of repetition, which in *Mikey and Nicky* is at once a narrative event, an organizing strategy, and an explicit theme. The two protagonists continually repeat themselves, muttering lines, names, and phrases to the point of exhaustion; the script, meanwhile, features multiple recurrences of a place, an image, an idea. Near the film's opening, for instance, Mikey appears at the door of Nicky's sleazy hotel room, banging to be let in. An identical action recurs several minutes later when he returns from an errand and is later reprised—if inverted—in the film's final sequence, when Nicky bangs with increasing urgency on Mikey's door. Mikey and Nicky retread the same streets, just as the hit man circles the block around Mikey's house; Nicky visits his mistress Nell's apartment once, then returns. The difficulty that doors present—the impossibility, in the final instance, of moving through them—is evocative of the kind of psychological blockage that besets both men.

Such repetition is not just a structuring feature of *Mikey and Nicky* but also a topic of discussion within it. "You called me the echo!" Mikey yells at Nicky during a climactic confrontation. "You tell everybody that I have to say everything twice because I got a tunnel in my head!" In the closing act of the film, Mikey returns to this preoccupation, asking his wife, Annie (played by Rose Arrick), "Do I repeat myself when I talk?" "Hmm?" she replies, surprised, prompting him, ironically, to repeat the question: "When I talk, do you hear me repeating myself?" "No!" she replies without much conviction. "Ever?" he presses. She shakes her head, smiling, and concedes, "Maybe, I never noticed it." "Well, notice it!" he says. "From now on, when I do something, notice it."

Mikey and Nicky is, among other things, an exercise in sustained noticing; it observes its characters with a relentlessness that can strike viewers as perverse, with scene length seemingly at odds with narrative significance. But there is something powerfully expressive about May's brand of realism, her refusal to streamline events and interactions for cinematic consumption. May herself intimated as much during a rare interview in 1975 in which she discussed the differences between lived experience and screen representation:

> I never realized how different movies are from life until I saw this movie [*Mikey and Nicky*], and I had this longing for a cliché. Any cliché. You usually know what's going to happen. And I realized that all movies have confrontation scenes in which, after the confrontation scene, something happens. And you realize that in life you have hundreds of confrontation scenes. Scenes in which you say the worst things you can say and in which you reveal yourself. And then, two hours later, you do it again. *And you do it over and over and over and over. There is no such thing as a single confrontation scene.* (Rivlin 84, italics mine)

Cliché, as May used it here, functions as narrative shorthand. *Mikey and Nicky*, by avoiding such shortcuts, produces something closer to the unpleasant redundancy of life, in which you do things "over and over and over and over." By May's own criteria, then, the film veers closer to lived experience, in which there is "no such thing as a single confrontation scene" and in which characters regularly "say the worst things [they] can say" and then, less than two hours later, "do it again."

This kind of hyperrealism deviates not just from the dominant regime of narrative cinema but also from storytelling conventions more broadly. In his analysis of frequency in prose fiction, for instance, Gérard Genette notes that "when . . . repeating phenomena occur in the story, the narrative is not by any means condemned to reproduce them in its discourse as if it were incapable of the slightest effort to abstract and synthesize: in fact, and except for deliberate stylistic effect, a narrative—and even the most unpolished one—will in this case find a sylleptic formulation such as 'every day,' or 'the whole week,' or [as in Proust, Genette's primary case study] 'every day of the week I went to bed early'" (116). Genette would famously describe such formulations, in which a "single narrative utterance takes upon itself several occurrences of the same event," as *iterative* (116). What makes *Mikey and Nicky* remarkable is its resistance to the iterative mode: to forms for narrative condensation that in film are typically accomplished via editing, voice-over, or dialogue. There is a noticeable absence of such "sylleptic" formula in *Mikey and Nicky*—which is to say, there is an absence of cliché. Instead, the film presents a case study in what Genette calls the *singulative*. It "reproduce[s] in its discourse" many instances of "repeating phenomena"; it makes little effort to "abstract and synthesize." The result is that viewers of *Mikey and Nicky* encounter life in all its unexpurgated frequencies. They experience—or feel they have been made to experience—each single iteration of a narrative event as a unique instance of patterns that May's characters are at once unable to discern and seemingly compelled to repeat.

The film establishes this dynamic early on when, as mentioned above, Mikey appears at the door of Nicky's room at the Hotel Royale. "It's Mikey from the corner. I came as soon as I got your towel," Mikey calls out, referring to the hand towel Nicky has thrown down in the street as a covert means of signaling his location. Faced with Nicky's paranoia, however, Micky must knock, cajole, and nearly kick down the door before his friend lets him in, all while repeating variations on a phrase with increasing volume and intensity: "Open the door, Nicky," "Schmuck, open the door!," "Open the door, Nick," "C'mon, open the door!," "Open the door, open it! Come on, Nick, open it up!" Once admitted, Mikey forces his clearly ailing friend to take medication for his ulcer, which he does, reluctantly. Mikey then leaves to procure half-and-half for Nicky's stomach, and when he returns, the drama of denied entry is reprised, with Mikey once again standing at the doorway, having to talk his way in. A similar degree of redundancy characterizes dialogue throughout the film, in which characters frequently repeat multiple variations of a phrase—"Open the door," "They're gonna kill me," "You're not gonna die," "Take it," "Don't go," "Let me out of the car"—with minimal impact or uptake.

In its commitment to exploring an action from every possible angle and reproducing interactions in all their inefficiency, *Mikey and Nicky* also reflects May's own impulses as a performer. May's creative stamina was a signature feature of her improvised comedy, as discussed above;

as Nichols put it, "She had endless capacity for invention. . . . She could go on and on in a character" (qtd. in Coleman 131). In her third film, to a visibly greater extent than in her first two comedies, duration becomes a similar mechanism for discovery, "go[ing] on and on" or doing it "over and over," the paradoxical means by which something original can emerge.

The evacuation of cliché—at the level of dialogue, camerawork, editing, and performance—is so complete as to undermine whatever expectations viewers might attach to the generic framework within which May works. The resulting volatility is such a pronounced feature of the film that it becomes notable within the diegesis. "You're like a maniac! All of a sudden you jump up, you're like a maniac!" Mikey yells at Nicky after he has sprinted out the door of the B&O Tavern and down the block, forcing his friend to give chase. In his commentary for the film's Criterion Collection release, Patton Oswalt remarked on the characters' instability, the fact that they operate on "absolute impulse, they don't know what they're going to do one second to the next." Significantly, neither do we. The sense of narrative unpredictability strongly present in May's two comedies resurfaces here in a darker key, the stakes of the film's *liveness* at once more pronounced and, given the subject matter, more urgent.

Compulsive Masculinity and 1970s American Cinema

In May's hands, the perverse realism of *Mikey and Nicky* doesn't just unsettle audience expectations. Whether or not May intended as much, it now registers as a rejoinder to the worshipful treatment of male outsiders that characterizes some of the most prominent examples of the buddy film, a genre ascendant in the 1970s.[55] In many canonical expressions of the genre, men might be as desperate as Mikey and Nicky, but they also enjoy consolations—rugged individualism, sexual liberation, social autonomy. As Jack Nicholson's character says to Dennis Hopper's hippie biker in *Easy Rider*, "What you represent to them is freedom."

By contrast, in *Mikey and Nicky*, masculinity doesn't connote freedom so much as it entails compulsion, a straitjacket that prevents breaking free or dropping out. *Mikey and Nicky*'s contribution to the discourse of masculinity in 1970s cinema, then, is to portray it as both compulsory and compulsive, one of the deeply gendered social scripts individuals inherit and, as in May's early play *Adaptation*, reflexively act out. The extent to which the film presents white American masculinity as an affliction is reflected in the characters' continual diagnoses of and attempted treatment of the other's ills, from Nicky's dyspepsia and bleeding ulcer to Mikey's echolalia. "I'm in trouble," Nicky says, the first full sentence spoken in the film; one of the last is "I'm sick, Mikey." "You know there's really something wrong with you?" Mikey tells Nicky at one point and then issues an even more pessimistic assessment: "You don't wanna feel better, you wanna die!" Their surroundings support this assessment. The Philadelphia cityscape, shot entirely at night (in Philadelphia and then Los Angeles as a stand-in), looks moribund; the interiors—Nell's apartment, Mikey and Annie's home, the B&O Tavern—seem airless. The movie theater and Black bar are notable exceptions, densely populated spaces possessed of a vitality entirely absent from the film's other venues. On balance, however, the film is dominated by unlovely images—drab interiors and unflattering close-ups of the main characters, who are shot, literally and figuratively, in an unforgiving light.

One way of watching *Mikey and Nicky* is as a series of set pieces showcasing the different flavors of male dysfunction. While commentary on the film to date has tended to emphasize the consequences of the two characters' behavior on each other, May seems at least as interested in the broader impact of their aggression on the movie's "minor" characters,

Figure 19. *Mikey and Nicky*: An unforgiving light   I

who are, not incidentally, nonmale, nonwhite, and/or working class. Mikey attacks the counterman in an all-night diner, while Nicky taunts a female bus passenger and assaults the driver after baiting some bar patrons with racist taunts. Both men slap Nell; Nicky roughs up his wife, Jan. Violence for both men is at once a default mode of relation and a means of self-definition; neither knows how to express himself in other than antagonistic terms. The extent to which their anger is displaced becomes clear in the cemetery sequence, when they voice the real source of anxiety: their fear that they "won't be anything . . . won't know anything." "You're a piece of nothing," Mikey tells Nicky, articulating his own paranoia that they are both functionally obsolete within the changing world order.

These scenes recall similar moments in contemporary 1970s cinema, which, significantly, also made a point of showcasing characters lashing out and punching down. The scene in which Mikey asks the waiter, with escalating hostility, for cream invites comparison to one of New Hollywood's best-known scenes: the moment in *Five Easy Pieces* when Jack Nicholson's character caps his increasingly belligerent requests for "wheat toast" with a sexist insult for the waitress ("I want you to hold it between your legs") and an explosive gesture of violence as he sweeps the plates and glassware from the table, then skips out on the bill. In *The Last Detail*, the main character, a sailor once again played by Jack Nicholson, lashes out at the bartender, who is unwilling to serve his underage friend. "I am the mother-fucking shore patrol!" he yells at the cowering man, then struts outside: "Did you see that cracker asshole?" Both outbursts are played at least partly for laughs; they are meant to signal the characters' iconoclasm and are justified within the narrative economies of both films as appropriate responses to the repressive systems from which these nonconformist characters seek to escape. The fallout for those on the receiving end of their aggression remains unconsidered. Such violent displays, viewers are made to understand, are just the by-product of the characters' outsized desires, the fantasies of flight—from exploitative jobs, clinging spouses, the military-industrial complex—according to which even death qualifies as a countercultural triumph, a final "fuck you," epitomized by the image of Peter Fonda and Dennis Hopper going out in a literal blaze of glory.

Figure 20. Reacting to violence

Mikey and Nicky shows no such deference to its characters' desires. Their violence is not absorbed by the narrative or excused with reference to characterization or plot. Instead, it remains marked, and the repercussions for the surrounding characters, a source of intense interest for the film. A fascinating case in point are the reactions of two Black female customers visible in the background of the diner scene; May has either directed or at the very least allowed the actors to react with evident amusement to Mikey's display of excessive force.

But the clearest evidence of this attention to aggression's specifically gendered consequences surfaces in the film's final third, during which Mikey and Nicky, having exhausted all other avenues, turn in desperation to women. In one of the film's most excruciating sequences, Nicky brings Mikey to visit his girlfriend, Nell, under the pretense that they will both "make it" with her. Once in her apartment, however, Nicky seduces Nell in plain view of Mikey and then—in a display of casual cruelty—tries to pimp out his clearly unwilling mistress to his friend. Cornered, Nell bites Nicky on the lip; humiliated, Mikey strikes Nell across the face. While many critics have attended to the film's harrowing content, McElhaney notes the way in which the film's discomfiting effects are amplified by its form: "For all the varied angles here . . . May still cuts within a 180-degree space, with the wide master shots of the apartment creating a proscenium-like theatrical environment. However, these shots do not work to comfortably 'ground' the spectator's perception. Instead, in their physical distance from the dramatic action, combined with the use of low-key lighting . . . the effect is of enormous spatial and dramatic tension."[56] There is also enormous ethical tension generated by the scene, which gives the audience no perspective with which they can comfortably align.

Heightening this discomfort is May's approach to time as well as space. The climax of the scene—Nell's debasement—feels both painfully inevitable and deliberately protracted. May's refusal to rush events is motivated, I'd suggest, by the desire not to minimize their impact on each character, perhaps especially Nell. The scene's affective charge is primarily conveyed through a complex network of reaction shots, which in turn further implicate the viewers in the scene's untenable emotional transactions. If the reaction shots in May's comedies are often used to mirror our own incredulous reactions to characters' behavior, in *Mikey and Nicky* our relation to the "reacting" characters is far less clear, and our identification is strongly compromised. Rather than producing relief by affirming our shared judgments with the characters on-screen, the pained reactions of Nell and Mikey in this scene generate agita as we are brought into unwelcome proximity to their experiences of shame and humiliation. Their discomfort, in short, produces our own. "I don't want you to see me like this," Nicky says to Mikey earlier in the film. But May's film repeatedly asks viewers to see characters at their worst.

The critical distance inherent in May's "dispassionate" or "reticent" approach, moreover, means that viewers are not offered ethical cues (McElhaney; Stevens, "Male Narrative"). May stages the scene in such a way as to give equal time to Nell's reactions as to Mikey's, and the editing and blocking keep all three characters continuously in play; the camera in this sequence is not more close to any one of the three characters. But she does pay careful attention to the beats of Nell's debasement, powerfully conveyed by Carol Grace's quiet performance. "Why do you treat me like this?" she asks in a small, earnest voice. "Don't you have any respect for me?" she murmurs, eyes downcast, through pursed lips. In her stunned passivity and meek protests, Nell is strikingly reminiscent of the title character in Barbara Loden's *Wanda*, who similarly suffers the abuse of the overbearing hustler, Mr. Dennis. Both Loden and May—dramatically different filmmakers in almost every regard—nonetheless make similar use of abjection: not as an

Figure 21. Nell: abjection as reflection

end in itself, as some feminist critics wrongly inferred in May's case, but as a reflection of the aggregated acts of cruelty that define many women's lives.

In its clear-eyed study of sexual politics, the scene actually echoes one of the earliest scenarios May wrote for the Compass Players some twenty years before. "Georgina's First Date" is, according to Janet Coleman, one of "several ruthlessly unsentimental studies" May produced during that time (111). In the sketch, the main character, Georgina, is so thrilled at the prospect of having a date for the prom that when the boy rapes her, she seems not to register the assault, so fully has she internalized the dehumanizing status quo. (Or, as May's scenario indicates, the character is "so absorbed in her own effort to have a 'personality,' that she is unaware of what she is being used for" [qtd. in Kercher 126]). It is, as May's collaborator Annette Hankin put it, an example of May's "overwhelmingly cool vision of truth and reality": "It was not a pretty vision. . . . I think she saw . . . love in a cruel light. It was a terrible, awesome vision, that of a person who has survived an emotional holocaust" (qtd. in Coleman 111). The result, as conveyed in the episode in Nell's apartment, constitutes as bleak a view of relations between men and women as any committed to cinema. As Elise Moore suggestively notes, "In *Mikey and Nicky*, all that's left of the scenes between men and women is discomfort, which seems to be, more than comedy, what May is after in her portrayals of gender." Or as Peter Falk put it more plainly, speaking of the film's disturbing implications, "It's not what you want, it's what exists, what is" ("Interview").

Like May's early scenario, what makes this sequence so singularly discomfiting isn't just the spectacle of the woman's humiliation; it's the character's active complicity in that humiliation. Femininity, it turns out, is no less toxic a regime. Gender roles in the universe of May's cinema and theater are akin to catastrophe, a set of disabling constraints imposed on human beings from birth. We hear Mikey brag about his young son's brawny size ("He's as big as a truck . . . beats up all the other kids in the nursery school"), while Nicky speaks of his infant daughter as yet another woman in his life ("She's mad at me, too . . . wouldn't hold my thumb"). Mikey, meanwhile, recounts the judgment he levied against his grieving parents as a small child for having reactions inappropriate to their gender: "My father cried, I remember. But my mother . . . she just sat there." Perhaps the most telling moment, however, is the throwaway comment Mikey's wife, Annie, delivers as they sit waiting for the hit man Mikey knows is approaching: "You ever go to one of those meetings at school? . . . They have sewing at school. The boys sew, the girls go to shop. You know? Because I guess you're not supposed to think that only women sew and only men carve." She seems to be making mindless conversation, yet the substance of her comments speaks to a more serious issue: the arbitrary bifurcation of human experience along gendered lines—sewing and carving, putting together and taking apart. The intractable nature of such divisions is apparent to Annie, who implies that you're "not supposed to think" they persist but who understands that they do. What ultimately distinguishes *Mikey and Nicky* from other thematically similar films of the decade, then, is that there is no refuge in antiheroic individualism—no escape from such complete social conditioning, from the childhoods that these characters never grew up from. Instead, the film shines a spotlight on the enduring damage caused by a life lived within gendered enclosures and the fallout of existing—as Mikey and Nicky have done—within such a segregated and emphatically violent milieu.

May's Writerly Style

An important sidebar to any discussion of *Mikey and Nicky* is the fact that the film has so often been dismissed as mere improvisation and the product of Falk and Cassavetes's genius to the exclusion of May's. In a telling anecdote, when the mayor of Philadelphia arranged a press event with *Mikey and Nicky*'s crew, May was literally overlooked until Falk explained that she—and not producer Michael Hausman—was the film's director.[57] Without denying the virtuosity of the film's performances or the fact that Falk and Cassavetes ad-libbed extensively during rehearsals and may even have contributed to the final script, it is important to state definitively that the rumors of *Mikey and Nicky*'s improvised status have been greatly exaggerated.[58] By all accounts, the film was carefully scripted and the product of singularly intense preparation and extensive direction on May's part. As her producer Julian Schlossberg affirmed in a recent interview, the "label of improvisation is totally unfair. . . . [E]very word was written by her," though he acknowledged that the film nonetheless possesses "an improvisational feeling" ("Commentary"). May herself, asked about the supposedly improvised nature of the film, dismissed the idea out of hand: "It's not possible to improvise this because—although it seems not to be—it's really plot-driven" (see the next section, "An Interview with Elaine May").

This is not to say that May did not allow or actively encourage improvisation during rehearsal, as she had on her previous films. According to Paramount publicist Tom Miller (writing under the pseudonym Tom Canford), Cassavetes called it "the tightest script he [ever] read," but that didn't keep the actors from riffing on it. As Cassavetes noted, "It's because we respect its tightness that we can play on it. She [May] would never ask that it always be done exactly the way she wrote it. Because something better might come out of it. A line, a quality, a mood" (qtd. in Canford 75). Producer Michael Hausman suggests that this experimentation on-set may have led to actual adjustments to the film. He described the script as "very soft butter. . . . [I]t was constantly changing" ("The Making"). Similarly, director of photography Victor Kemper confirmed that Falk and Cassavetes were "consistent about not sticking to the script. . . . [T]hey ad-libbed everywhere, every time," but he didn't distinguish between rehearsals and filmed takes—a line that times became blurred ("The Making"). According to crew members, May "filmed her rehearsals, fearful she would lose an inspired bit of spontaneity if she did not, some great piece of business, some expression that might not be recaptured on succeeding takes" (Canford 76). But there were limits to such exploration, and Cassavetes recalled a note delivered to him during production by May's assistant: "Elaine says learn the lines" (qtd. in Canford 75).

More interesting than whether actors' ad-libbed lines made it into the film, however, is the impression of spontaneity that May managed to cultivate within the fixed bounds of a script that, by all accounts, she had been writing and rewriting since her earliest days with the Compass Players. Brad Stevens is the critic most alert to this tension within the film and the fact that its shambolic surface only "seems to put up . . . resistance to any kind of formalist reading" ("Male Narrative" 76). What might initially scan as "an undisciplined exercise in improvisation," then, is actually revealed to be a more controlled experiment; as Stevens suggests, "May has deliberately adopted the surface characteristics of this style in order to allow her audience to react more directly" and concludes that "repeated viewings of the film reveal that May's mise-en-scène is in fact highly sophisticated, and that the impression of stylelessness actually enables her to achieve the stylistic effects which would otherwise affect us intellectually but not emotionally" (76). Even if the film betrays less obvious curation than May's first two films, then, it is through *Mikey and Nicky*'s apparent artlessness that its artistry ultimately inheres.

Stevens's reference to "repeated viewings" is especially telling, since it highlights both the comparatively latent aspect of May's formalism in the film and the degree to which that formalism may only become manifest to viewers through more active and motivated viewing. In this sense, one could go so far as to classify *Mikey and Nicky* as what Roland Barthes would call a *writerly* text, one that is produced in the act of reading—or viewing—and that, compared to the only somewhat more "readerly" comedies May had previously created, invites a new (and for some audiences, perhaps undesirable) degree of engagement.[59]

Invites but also rewards. Almost every testimonial or firsthand description from the cast and crew reflects the extraordinary degree of care May took with every aspect of the film's production, from set design, to performance, to the extended editing process. Editor Sheldon Kahn, for one, described her absolute command of the film during the edit: "Elaine has a photographic memory. If we cut a scene thirteen ways, she'd go, 'The third way was the best.' She'd then recall it frame by frame" (qtd. in Abramowitz 80). May came by her investment honestly; her inspiration for the story was personal.[60] May herself confirmed this in a conversation with Haden Guest: "The milieu, the people in this movie, are actually my milieu. I'm a Chicago, sort of gangster girl. And the events aren't exactly true, but they have happened. So it's kind of a true story, but nobody knows this about me except you guys, and I'm afraid you all have to die" (see the next section, "An Interview with Elaine May"). It was a story, as mentioned, that May had been working on since at least her Compass Players days, as Peter Cooper, in an unlicensed book-length appreciation of the film, correctly notes: "You have to consider that the film had been brewing in her mind for 20 years. She had it all worked out" (16). When Paramount publicist Tom Miller hazarded the possibility that May was acting like a director "who hasn't got a clue as to what they're ultimately up to," Cassavetes quickly corrected him: "She knows. Believe me, she knows" (qtd. in Canford 17).

The set design reflects May's meticulous attention to detail. Some of her interventions have become lore, like the time she asked the crew, during one of the 110 night-for-night shots they lit, to restring the lights so that the characters could walk in the other direction ("The Making"). When it came time to shoot the film's climactic scenes, a physical confrontation between Mikey and Nicky, "May decided to change things. She wanted to scrap South Street entirely and contained the whole thing along two blocks of Front Street. That meant not only moving the lights and putting up more fake storefronts, but she also asked them to pave a couple of blocks of the infamously bumpy Front Street" (Cooper 144–45). For the scenes at the Hotel Royale, meanwhile, May had crew members redesign the lobby of the Essex Hotel, "making it smaller and adjusting the location of the lobby stairs" (16). Other gestures were somewhat more restrained. In Nicky's hotel room, she had the walls covered with Vaseline and plaster to enhance the "old diaper color" she was looking for (17). And in the diner scene, May carefully positioned the donuts displayed on the plate: "When she finally thought it was perfect, she paced [sic] the plate of doughnuts on the counter where it would be in the forefront of the shot and put a plastic orange cover over the plate. She looked at the plate through the camera. What she saw did not please her. She removed the cover and looked again, still dissatisfied" (Canford 85). Cooper compares May's adjustments to "Kubrick arranging cans of Calumet baking powder in the Overlook's pantry for *The Shining*" (Cooper 27). It is an auspicious comparison not because May and Kubrick share much in common as filmmakers but because "perfectionism" has historically had a far more positive connotation when associated with male directors.

Such actions, by all accounts, were nearly always undertaken in the service of performance. May thought the donuts in the diner scene, for instance, "might suggest something" to Falk, as assistant director Pete Scoppa affirmed; "then again he may ignore them" (qtd. in Canford 86).[61] Similarly, May furnished the entire apartment in which Mikey and Nicky meet Nell, even though the shoot would only take place in a single room. As Carol Grace told a *Chicago Tribune* reporter covering the film's production, "There were toiletries in the medicine chest, dishes in the cabinet, and food in the refrigerator" (Rottenberg). One of May's assistants at the time affirmed that such measures are "not an extravagance. . . . It's important to Elaine that people in the film feel what they are doing is real" (Rottenberg). That's not to say, of course, that May wasn't also opportunistic. When Falk slipped while running through the hotel lobby, May used the take; she similarly included a shot from the characters' conversation in the cemetery in which a small microphone is visible on Falk's tie. Then, when Victor Kemper temporarily quit, she took Cassavetes up on his offer to take over, with apparently negligible results. (When they reviewed the footage he had shot, "all they saw was a black screen. They couldn't make out anything" [Cooper 165].) More successful were the behavioral touches both actors apparently brought to their roles. When the two men sat in the B&O Tavern, for instance, Cassavetes diverged from the stage directions that "NICK sits drumming his fingers on the table" (May, *Mikey and Nicky* 29), instead improvising a series of smaller gestures: "The smoke rings, the wide-eyed look, and the mock choking all came out during filming" (Cooper 61). But on the whole, even these "accidents" exist within the context of May's direction.

The film's use of red provides a particularly vivid example of the kind of creative intervention that only reveals itself through close attention and may also reflect the input of Anthea Sylbert, who is credited as "visual consultant" on *Mikey and Nicky*, as well as her then husband, Paul Sylbert, who served as the film's art director (and with whom May would reteam, albeit acrimoniously, on *Ishtar*). In *Mikey and Nicky*, the color red appears in nearly every space the two characters inhabit.

Figure 22. Seeing red

It shows up in the B&O Tavern in its neon sign, pinball machine, and Coke and beer bottles; in clothing such as Nicky's tie, the cuff of Mikey's son's pajamas, and the sweater worn by the bar patron Nicky hits on; in the interior accents of the bus and the facade of the movie theater; and, most conspicuously, in the bright red wall of Nell's apartment. What looks like a mere motif acquires significance not in an overt, Sirkian way, then, but in a subtler one. In addition to adding interest to *Mikey and Nicky*'s grim nocturnal palate, the color's ubiquity becomes a visual reminder of violence's persistence in the world of the film, the extent to which the film's subjects are always "seeing red," regardless of the particular space they occupy.

It is one example of the way in which meaning in *Mikey and Nicky* accrues in the aggregate through the accumulation of shots rather than any one shot. It can be hard to "quote" from the film for this reason or to find a single image that seems representative. Again and again, May tests the limits of the scene as a constitutive unit of cinema, "begin[ning] and end[ing] in what would be the middle in a more conventional film," much as Marshall Fine has written of Cassavetes (260), or, conversely, letting a scene continue beyond the point of narrative necessity. Significantly, though May is seldom compared to her avant-garde contemporaries, *Mikey and Nicky* shares not only with Cassavetes but also with other, more experimental filmmakers of the period a resistance to narrative condensation. It's a film that must be experienced and that is strongly differentiated from the "high-concept" mandate of the 1980s that May herself would have to contend with in making *Ishtar*.

Meaning also accrues in the many extratextual decisions May made, particularly when it comes to casting. In addition to recruiting Falk and Cassavetes—friends who had worked together previously—May was extremely strategic about casting the film's smaller roles. Perhaps most shocking was that May had originally convinced Frank Yablans— then the president of Paramount—to play the role of the hit man. The studio, not surprisingly, nixed the plan, and the part would eventually go to Ned Beatty. But what persists is the analogy, clearly established in May's mind, between assassins and industry executives.[62] Along similar lines, May invited Elia Kazan to play the role of the mob boss; according to May, he responded, "I'll do it if I can play the killer" (see the next section, "An Interview with Elaine May"). Ultimately, the part would go to Sanford Meisner, the legendary acting teacher and an American disseminator of the Method, a decision with different but no less fascinating implications. By casting as criminals some of the era's most celebrated practitioners and teachers of this muscular new form of acting—Falk, Cassavetes, and Meisner—May set up a world in which revered figures play, in May's words, "little businessmen" (see the next section, "An Interview with Elaine May"). Along similar lines, Carrie Rickey suggests that May's casting of Meisner and fellow acting teacher

Figure 23. The acting mob I

William Hickey in the role of mafiosi set up an implicit parallel between New York's "acting mob" and the actual mob.

This is not to imply that May harbored any disrespect toward her actors, but it is to suggest that she used casting as an expressive device and a potent, if somewhat elliptical, rhetorical tool. In a 2010 discussion following a screening of *Mikey and Nicky* at the Harvard Film Archive, May called Falk and Cassavetes "perfect for the part" due to their long-standing intimacy and real-life friendship, which heightened the intensity of their on-screen rapport. But contributing to their "perfection," too, may well have been the public personae they brought to their roles (see the next section, "An Interview with Elaine May").

May repeated this strategy with the casting of *Ishtar* roughly ten years later. Like Falk and Cassavetes, Warren Beatty and Dustin Hoffman were "perfect" for their parts, inasmuch as they enabled May to engineer a world in which legendary men could play schlubs and hacks. Paradoxically, given the historical deprecation of May's craft on the film, it was precisely her originality and uncompromising vision on *Mikey and Nicky* that exposed her to the tactics of the Hollywood mob, with whom she would famously battle over the film's final cut, going so far as to have a friend of her then husband, David Rubenfine (as the story goes), smuggle a reel of the film out of state and keep it hidden from Paramount.[63] But it was only with her fourth and final film, *Ishtar*, that May would truly become the target of an industry hit.

Ishtar: Trolling Hollywood

In 1959 Elaine May and Mike Nichols performed a routine for the live broadcast of the Emmy Awards. In it, May walks out to the podium, looking around with an air of studied seriousness, and begins her speech. "There will be much said here tonight about excellence, and the creative, the skillful, and the artistic will all be recognized and rewarded," she says. "But what of the others in this industry?" The room, after a beat, erupts into laughter. "Seriously," she continues without breaking character. "There are men in the industry who go on, year in and year out, quietly and unassumingly producing garbage." Having provided the set-up, she announces that she is here tonight to present the evening's "special award to the man who has been voted 'the most total mediocrity' in the industry, Lyle Glass!" Then Mike Nichols, all smiles, rises from the audience and bounds up to the stage to accept his award. He thanks the Academy and expresses pride in himself for "sticking to my one ideal: money" and ignoring the appeals of his staff that he "try and do something good." He credits his success to three additional factors: taking all the sponsors' suggestions, endeavoring to "offend no one anywhere on Earth," and "disregard[ing] talent in order to hire only 'swell guys.'"

The routine is both a sterling piece of comedy and a withering critique of the American television industry. But as it happens, it is also an illuminating intertext for May's final film, *Ishtar* (1987), which is similarly concerned with the spectacle of white male mediocrity. If this early sketch skewered the gender politics of television production, which enabled men to "go on . . . quietly and unassumingly producing garbage," *Ishtar* was born of May's interest in the broader consequences of a culture that has made a business out of empowering "swell guys." As May commented in a 2006 conversation with Nichols, "When I made [*Ishtar*] Ronald Reagan was president . . . and I remember looking at [him] and thinking . . . he's from Hollywood. He's a really nice man. It's possible that the only movies he's ever seen about the Middle East are the *Road* movies with Hope and Crosby. And I thought, I would make that movie" ("Elaine May in Conversation"). The result is not only a prescient satire of 1980s US foreign policy.[64] Within the film's plot-level send-up of American "intelligence" also lurks a latent critique of Hollywood and the industry's long-standing role in peddling fantasies about Western innocence and heroic masculinity, fantasies *Ishtar* toys with, upends, and deflates.[65] Threaded through almost every aspect of the film's production, from its casting to its framing, editing, and visual style, is an insider's assessment of show business as usual sly enough to qualify as trolling.

For the uninitiated, *Ishtar* follows the fate of two hopelessly untalented songwriters, Lyle Rogers and Chuck Clark, who find themselves at the center of a geopolitical crisis in the Middle East after their agent, Marty Freed (played by Jack Weston), books them a gig in Morocco. That many people remain uninitiated is a legacy of the film's long-standing reputation as a notorious flop; as May quipped, "If all the people who hate *Ishtar* had seen it, I would be a rich woman" ("Elaine

May in Conversation"). The story of how *Ishtar* became a cultural punch line will be discussed in greater detail below. But one of the many consequences of *Ishtar*'s postrelease fate is that it has remained an object of fascination more than analysis. While *Ishtar* has seen its reputation refurbished in recent years, the film has still attracted less sustained attention from scholars. That much of the commentary that does exist accepts *Ishtar*'s failure as an article of faith, moreover, makes it arguably more important to offer a positive accounting of May's final film.

At the same time, it is important not to misrepresent May's ambitions in making *Ishtar*, a film that emerged at the height of the blockbuster era, in which "high concept" logics had superseded the auteurist mandate of the previous decade.[66] On the one hand, one could say that *Ishtar*, despite its substantially bigger budget and profile, simply scaled the method of her early comedies, using lighthearted farce as the vehicle for her deflationary project. Once again May displays a knack for co-opting Hollywood's conventions, pitching her blistering satire as a riff on the blandly predictable *Road to Morocco* (1942) and casting two of the industry's most bankable stars, Warren Beatty and Dustin Hoffman, aggressively against type. While May's male peers distinguished themselves as cinephiles and students of classical Hollywood, *Ishtar*, a decade later, reflects an entirely ironic engagement with the industry's idols and archetypes. May has made little secret of her irreverence, noting offhandedly in 2010, "I don't think any funny movies were really funny until about 1980. I watch old movies and I cannot understand what's funny about them" (see the next section, "An Interview with Elaine May").

Yet if *Ishtar* can be seen as an auteurist statement, it was also designed as a commercial entertainment, one that could compete in the cutthroat arena of 1980s Hollywood. In fact, one could easily choose to approach the film from just this angle and to self-select into what Peter Rabinowitz calls the "gullible" rather than the "discerning" authorial audience (203). Indeed, when it comes to *Ishtar*, it can be hard to tell with certainty what or even whether one *is* discerning. That one of *Ishtar*'s two dim-witted protagonists shares the name "Lyle" with the sham awardee of Nichols and May's routine, for instance, could be mere coincidence. Then again, it may be a name May invokes as a shorthand for cluelessness and one of the many subtle ways she embedded her commentary on America's seemingly boundless capacity for self-deceit into a mainstream studio comedy. As May herself would put it, "The film was political and it was a satire but it was my secret" ("Elaine May in Conversation").

In short, *Ishtar* may be best understood as both a product of Hollywood and a response to it, a look back at classical and postclassical tropes and a reappraisal of them. In this sense, it's possible to understand May's final film—in the language of Rogers and Clark's best-known song—as at once honest *and* popular, if only aspirationally so. That *Ishtar* didn't achieve popularity may be, if only in small part, the product of its bifurcated ambitions.

The Bathos of Failure

If *Ishtar* trolls the desultory qualities of "old" Hollywood comedy, it also takes a skeptical stance toward the excesses of New Hollywood. Particularly revealing in this regard is the film's waggish focus on failed masculine ambition, a theme 1970s cinema had essentially fetishized. In his essay "The Pathos of Failure: American Films in the 1970s," Thomas Elsaesser examines "the unmotivated hero of the American Cinema" and the "motif of the journey" that supplies the missing motive power, which in these films assumes the "blander status of a narrative device" or a "pretext to keep the film moving" (280, 279). Taking as his case studies road movies such as *Two-Lane Blacktop* (1971), *Five Easy Pieces* (1970), *The Last Detail* (1971), and *Easy Rider* (1969), Elsaesser argues that these films upended Hollywood's ideological presets, converting the "a priori optimism" associated with forward movement into radical skepticism, such that "the road comes to stand for the very quality of contingency" (281). Though Elsaesser describes the approach of the 1970s "anti-action" film as "unsentimental," there is no denying the lingering affection with which even the most caustic of these films regard the sum of their semantic parts: not only their alienated protagonists, "rebels and outsiders" all, but also the iconography—classic cars, open roads, sweeping vistas, chrome diners, beat-up denim, country girls— that surrounds them and the generally picturesque or grandly beautiful regional spaces through which they move (282). Indeed, Elsaesser implies as much in the title of the essay, which alludes to the pathos inherent in these fallen heroes navigating fallen worlds.

Ishtar was made fully fifteen years after many of the films in this bracket and would seem—between its antic comedy and hypermotivated protagonists—to have little to do with the phenomenon Elsaesser describes. Yet it, too, is a road movie, as much as a *Road* movie, just one that May has opportunistically reshaped for her own purposes. (Nichols, in his conversation with May, acknowledged as much, saying, "It's true, this is a road movie, about the Middle East" ["Elaine May in Conversation"].) As she did in *Mikey and Nicky*, May riffs on the cultural fetish for male dysfunction, giving us, in place of renegades possessed of rugged good looks, two "aging nonentities" in khaki pants (Kael, "Noodles" 102). When the pair does hit the road, they head the wrong way—east, not west—and go in circles (see their ride atop a blind camel). *Ishtar*, in this sense, effectively calls New Hollywood's bluff, making the spectacle of men flailing and failing the stuff of farce, not naturalistic drama. In short, one could say that May converts the pathos of the 1970s antihero into the bathos of the hapless schmuck.

Put another way, *Ishtar* brings a lightness of touch to the spectacle of men's personal and creative failure, subjecting it to fresh comic scrutiny. In an opening montage, May introduces Chuck Clark and Lyle Rogers, played by Dustin Hoffman and Warren Beatty, friends and cofounders of a musical duo known as Rogers and Clark, by offering a "behind-the-scenes" look at their creative process. Gathered around a piano in Chuck's apartment, the two characters at first evoke a Brill Building team, but as we listen to them spit-ball lyrics for a new song, it's clear the caliber of their work is subprofessional: "Telling the truth is a *difficult problem*," "Telling the truth is a *scary predicament*," "Telling the truth is a *bitter herb*." ("Forget 'herb'! I never heard of a hit that had the word 'herb' in it," Chuck snaps.) May cuts to a shot of the two men staring through the window of a record store at a Simon and Garfunkel album. "'Dangerous Business' is as good as anything they ever wrote," Clark insists. The audience knows better. Like the rest of the diegetic soundtrack, "Dangerous Business" is the result of May's collaboration with Paul Williams, who wrote the music for such believably "bad" songs as "Wardrobe of Love," "That a Lawn Mower Can Do All That," and "I Look to Mecca." (May, it should be noted, wrote many of the lyrics.) The pace and editing of these early scenes are remarkably brisk yet entirely precise; nothing is rushed or abstracted. Instead, *Ishtar* takes the first twenty minutes to showcase Chuck and Lyle's creative process and its desultory results, delaying the start of the "road" plot so as to procedurally document, in almost loving detail (or, in May's words, "step by tiny step"), the doing of something very badly in almost real time.

Though Hollywood cinema had featured any number of wannabe artists in films as varied as *Kiss Me Stupid* (1964), *King of Comedy* (1982), or the partly May-penned *Tootsie* (1986), few directors have mined the comic potential of artistic mediocrity quite so fully. Indeed, it's the characters' commitment to their craft—however misguided—that partly redeems them in the film's eyes. Chuck and Lyle at least have the virtue of aiming for artistry *as well as* commercial success, differentiating them from the craven studio men Nichols and May lampooned in their Emmy Awards sketch. As Shira Assel (Isabelle Adjani), the insurgent rebel leader who also serves as the men's shared romantic interest, tearfully concludes in the final scene, "I think they're wonderful." Yet it's clearly an ironic assessment, and *Ishtar*'s gentle treatment of its protagonists stops short of an encompassing humanism. The closest May gets is to allow them brief moments of self-awareness, as when Chuck, threatening suicide, confides to Lyle, "I've been fooling you, Lyle, and I've been fooling myself. I don't have any talent and I don't have any money. . . . I'm a total failure." Yet this flash of insight is almost immediately undermined by Chuck's plea that Lyle not call the police so as to protect his (nonexistent) career prospects. ("If this gets into the newspapers, the scandal will ruin me in show business!")

Impending tragedy undercut by comedy, pathos converted into bathos—anticlimax is a recurring feature of *Ishtar*. Chuck's suicide attempt becomes a de facto family reunion, complete with rabbi, trying to coax him back off the ledge; a deadly shootout in the desert ends with the discharge of an absurdly large grenade-launcher; the stakes of Ishtari independence are trivialized by Lyle's discovery that its guerrilla leader has breasts. If *Mikey and Nicky* envisioned white American masculinity as a Beckettian affliction—a dark night of the soul—in *Ishtar* it's more like a running joke. It's the film that makes most explicit May's long-standing interest in male idiocy, epitomized by the scene in which Lyle, depressed by the recent departure of his wife, sadly murmurs, "I'm such a smuck." "*Shmuck*," Chuck corrects him. "Smuck," Lyle repeats. Chuck takes a beat: "Say 'shhhh.' . . . [N]ow say 'muck.' . . . [N]ow say 'shh' and 'muck' together real fast." "Smuck," Lyle says. Chuck pauses, then gives his friend a consoling pat on the shoulder: "Closer," he nods.

In deflating pop culture's fascination with tortured masculinity, *Ishtar* is commensurate with May's broader body of work. "Most men lead lives of quiet desperation," Chuck solemnly tells Lyle, quoting (but not crediting) Thoreau. It's the kind of line that recurs across May's stage plays, such as *Taller Than a Dwarf*, whose self-aggrandizing protagonist peddles similarly derivative wisdom. When Lyle later talks Chuck down off both the metaphorical and the literal ledge, he offers his own brand of Yogi Berra–ism, almost profound in its stupidity: "It takes a lot of nerve to have nothing at your age . . . You'd rather have nothing than settle for less!" Like many of May's subsequent plays, *Ishtar* suggests that men's ambitions may often outstrip their abilities.

As in *Mikey and Nicky*, in *Ishtar* the characters' interactions with others—including women and children—make their insensibility most visible. Lyle, who drives a Good Humor truck, is so absorbed in finding a rhyme for his new song ("hot fudge love . . . cherry ripple kisses . . . delicious . . . knishes . . . ") that he fails to hear his young would-be customers running alongside, begging him to stop. Both he and Chuck betray utter narcissism where their romantic partners are concerned. Early in the film, Chuck's girlfriend (played by Carol Kane) tells Chuck that she loves him. "Thanks," he responds, distractedly. Meanwhile, in

Figure 24. Long-suffering women |

an earlier scene, Lyle sits banging away on his keyboard, oblivious to his wife Willa's frustration. Notably, a previous version of the *Ishtar* script contains an extended version of their exchange, in which Willa voices her thwarted ambitions while her husband noodles away on guitar, making his childlike self-absorption even more explicit:

WILLA
I want to be an interior decorator.
(Lyle blinks)
I want a career. I got talent, Lyle. I know it. I want to *do* something with my life.
LYLE
Okay.
WILLA
I want to enroll in the Pratt Institute of Design.
LYLE
Okay.
WILLA
It costs seven hundred dollars.
LYLE
Seven hundred dollars?
(Slowly)
Well . . . we got money saved.
WILLA
That means no piano.
LYLE
Well, hell, Willa, you got just as much right to a career as I do. I'll just learn to play this [guitar] better! (May, *Ishtar* 11)

Even when it's explained to him, Lyle still doesn't get it. But Willa's response—to burst into tears because Lyle is "so nice to [her]"—suggests that, as in May's other films, men don't have a monopoly on risible behavior (12).

The result is an ironic distance from all of *Ishtar*'s characters that is crucial to the creation of satire, a mode that "requires observation and judgement rather than identification" (Kolker 113, qtd. in King 103). It's an orientation that, as Geoff King further notes, is "rarely found in Hollywood or other film comedy in the commercial mainstream," making May's commitment to observational detachment in a big-budget production such as *Ishtar* especially notable (103).[67] Without distancing us from her main characters' subjectivity, May simultaneously draws on a theatrical aesthetic regime to create what might be called a partial alienation effect. Far from "identifying" with these characters but without insisting on estrangement, May's observational approach suggests that access to these men does not constitute an endorsement.

Staging Satire

Compared to May's previous films, *Ishtar*'s visual rhetoric is neither as distinctive nor as definitive in terms of mediating viewers' relationship to the characters. Apart from the briskly paced opening montage—a hallmark of all of May's comedies—*Ishtar*'s most notable features may be its reliance on master shots rather than on shot / reverse shot editing patterns. Dean Brandum similarly discerned this tendency in a discussion of *Ishtar*'s aesthetics, noting that "the standard master-two-shot-reverse-shot progression is often reduced to only the master within a stationary frame" (148).[68] While Brandum may overstate the consistency of the film's "grammar," which is more variegated than this characterization suggests, it is true that *Ishtar* tends to hold shots "long after others would cut," a choice that helps to amplify a scene's "comic possibilities" by placing emphasis on performance and character work (148).

The comparatively understated nature of the film's camera work is itself remarkable, given that May was working with Vittorio Storaro, an Italian cinematographer known for such spectacular productions as *The Conformist* (1970) and *Apocalypse Now* (1979). But there is more to be said about the rhetorical effects of *Ishtar*'s muted visual syntax—specifically, about its debts to May's improvisational comedy. While Brandum alludes to the "proscenium arch effect" produced by May's static takes, less noted have been the parallels between this approach and the staging of her comic routines with Nichols (Brandum 148).[69] Both their televised and live performances, for instance, involved the pair sitting side by side or in close proximity to each other on a stage, shot by a single camera in a single take, with no reliance on editing or camera movement. While the routines featured costumes, makeup, and minimal props, they largely relied on Nichols and May's precisely calibrated use of gesture and facial expression, with the sketches driven, above all, by spoken dialogue, as attested by their comedy's successful translation to audio recordings. (There's a reason so many comics, from Tom Lehrer to Steve Martin, recall having listened to Nichols and May's albums "over and over again" [Nachman 321].) May's films, much like her performances, similarly lead with the delivery of precisely honed dialogue, and *Ishtar*, as Sam Wasson observes, "more than her previous films . . . was full of crafted jokes" (297).

A case in point is the scene in which Chuck meets with Jim Harrison, the CIA agent (played by Charles Grodin) trying to recruit the two hapless Americans. The scene's setting in a North African restaurant allows for visual gags—as when Chuck, asked disingenuously by Jim for an autograph, first needs to wipe couscous off his fingers. But the scene's humor is carried by the dialogue, with Jim sharing casually, in response to Chuck's inquiry about his line of work, that he's "with the CIA." Having described the agency's recruitment process, which involves weekly payouts to informers, he concludes sanctimoniously, "You can't put a price on democracy." "Yeah, but $150 is a pretty good start," Chuck replies. Later encounters between Chuck and Jim—at a romantic, candle-lit table for two and then in a camel market—similarly rely on medium two-shots, suggesting the consistency with which *Ishtar* is staged and shot to prioritize two-way dialogue and performance. In this sense, May's film aligns with the commitments of the screwball comedy, in which "the prominence of 'talk,'" as Sarah Kozloff writes, "leads to an understated, but by no means inartistic, visual style" (170).

At the same time, it's worth noting that this approach contravenes long-standing "cinematic" logics that prioritize montage over staging and visual storytelling over the use of words. If film comedy has labored under the expectation that it "benefits from a zero-degree style," then filmmakers in general must still contend with what David Bordwell describes as the deprecation of "staging-driven cinema" and an entrenched bias against dialogue (Morrison 115; Bordwell 8).[70] Indeed, these critical tendencies make it easier to understand how May's approach might have been summarily dismissed. Happily, more recent assessments of May's work reflect a greater appreciation for her style. Chad Perman, for one, calls *Ishtar* a "comedy of accumulation, of unexpected choices and narrative beats that eventually turn a standard set-up into a surreal playground where anything goes," while Brad

Stevens observes that "[m]any of *Ishtar*'s most delightful moments are observed via long, meticulously composed takes which enable the performers to interact with each other and the world around them" ("*Ishtar*").

In one example of May's progressively building comedy, Chuck collapses during the pair's forced march through the desert. The following two-minute scene develops through a series of visual gags and one-liners. As Lyle army-crawls toward his friend's prone body, he shoos a vulture away from Chuck, hissing, "Not dead, just resting!" When Chuck revives and notices one particularly assertive specimen eyeing him, he murmurs, "You mean he's here on spec?" The situational comedy created by the men's obviously deficient reaction to their predicament is further amplified, as in May's first two comedies, by ironic flourishes within the frame. "I think it's really important not to let yourself get run down out here," Lyle offers as vultures race back and forth across the screen, the desert stretching endlessly into the background.

It's a scene that has clearly been optimized for laughs, not visual spectacle, an approach that created tension on the set, especially with Storaro, who was "designing shots with an eye to their composition, their beauty, whereas [May] was composing for comic effect" (Biskind, *Star* 351). Many of May's detractors, however, seem unable to accept that she *was* composing—that hers was an approach, just one that didn't necessarily align with the expectations of her crew or with critical consensus.[71]

Figure 25. Optimized for laughs, not
visual spectacle

In fact, this scene—and Lyle's absurd recourse to platitudes in a moment of extremis—underscores the continuities between May's working methods and her two-handed comedy with Nichols. In both contexts, dialogue reflects beliefs about language indebted to the work of early twentieth-century theorist Mikhail Bakhtin: namely, the idea that even individual utterances are circumscribed by social forces in the form of "speech genres." It's a concept continually in play in Nichols and May's routines, which make extensive use of generic utterances—especially "yes, and"—and get comic mileage from the invocation of overworked phrases, bureaucratese, and jargon. (One example appears in "Bach to Bach," in which a postcoital couple riffs on the terms "relating" and "relationship": "Oh, we didn't *relate*. There was proximity but no *relating*" [Nichols and May, *Improvisations*].)[72] In *Ishtar*, Beatty's conversation is strewn with affirmative formulas ("Oh, is that true!," "Oh, is that right!"), while Adjani's employs the heightened rhetoric of a melodrama. "It means my life," she says, begging Chuck to return the missing map that serves as the film's MacGuffin. "That means your life, too?" he responds. Meanwhile, her instructions to Lyle ("Go to the camel market in Shalibenima. . . . [A]sk for Muhammad. . . . [T]ell him you want to buy a *blind camel*") recall Nichols and May's play on the language of Cold War spycraft in their sketch "Mysterioso" (*Improvisations*). In *Ishtar*, as in so much of Nichols and May's comedy, language draws attention to itself as a construction, not a naturalistic occurrence. If *Ishtar* feels at times like a series of set pieces—a collection of Nichols and May routines—it is arguably a strength of the film, not a drawback, one that reflects a dialogue-driven approach to comedy that may be profilmic as much as it is narrowly "cinematic."

Hollywood Gimmicks

No one may have understood the tendency of May's vision to deviate from default "cinematic" parameters better than May herself, as an early scene implies. In it, Chuck and Lyle's newly hired agent, Marty Freed, sits them down after their set. Asked for feedback, he levels with them. "You're old, you're white, you got no shtick. You got no gimmick!" As he talks, Chuck self-consciously pulls some of his hair from behind the bandana he has tied around his head, as if he is just for the first time reckoning with the duo's lack of curb appeal. At their next show,

Figure 26. "Sing songs people know"

he and Lyle—attempting to take Marty's advice to "sing songs people know" so that they will always have "something to applaud"—perform the Diamonds' "Little Darlin,'" complete with hackneyed dance moves and Lyle's stiff-backed bongo playing, to the stupefaction of the crowd.

Chuck and Lyle's attempts to pander to the audience end in spectacular failure, exposing the limits of Marty's cynical show-biz values and the idea that gimmickry can compensate for a lack of talent. Then again, Rogers and Clark receive rapturous applause at the Chez Casablanca when they accede to the crowd's demands for novelty tunes such as "That's Amore!" *Ishtar*, then, is at once coruscating and clear-eyed on the subject of commercialism, the crowd-pleasing mandates that govern mainstream film and music production. It's an issue May had navigated in her own work; by many accounts, including Nichols's, she ended their partnership at least in part because his careerist ambitions diverged from her more purely creative ones. As Nichols put it, "She was more interested in taking chances than in being a hit. I was more interested in making the audience happy" (qtd. in Harris 109).

Significantly, the perils of pandering are made most visible in a sequence from an earlier version of *Ishtar*'s script that was evidently cut from the final film. As originally written, Chuck and Lyle take to heart Marty's advice "to put in more jokes" and perform a new extended set that intersperses attempts at live comedy with "a four-handed version of 'American Pie'" (6). All the jokes, however, are sexist, anti-Semitic cracks about Jewish American princesses ("What's a Jewish princess's favorite wine?" "I wanna go to Miami!"), leading women in the audiences to revolt (6). "Why don't you do some jokes about men?" one calls out (6). "How many assholes does it take to do an act?" another shouts (7). The MC tries to appease the crowd: "I wasn't here when this act was screened, and I'm sorry for its tastelessness" (8). The duo ends with a joke that compares Jewish women's performance in bed unfavorably to Jell-O ("Jell-O moves") (8). "Fuck you!" a woman responds (8). Without knowing the reason for this scene's omission, it's worth noting that the excised scene would have represented by far the film's most explicit rebuke of both show business's profit-seeking motives and its casual misogyny.

Perhaps the most persuasive case for reading *Ishtar* as a critique of Hollywood's bottom-line thinking, however, lies in its intertextual relationship to the *Road* movies and the fact that May took the most frankly commercial of conceits, a tried-and-true Hollywood formula, as her point of departure. Even those fans of *Road to Morocco* would concede that the film was a studio product and star vehicle, allowing Paramount to capitalize on its earlier entries in the Hope-Crosby-Lamour franchise, *Road to Singapore* (1940) and *Road to Zanzibar* (1941). Many of the most "dated" and now cringe-inducing aspects of *Ishtar,* after all—namely, the infantile sexual humor and Islamophobia—are standbys from *Road to Morocco.* In its riff of this formula, *Ishtar* draws attention to some of its key drawbacks: the original film's songs were forgettable (despite the talents of Johnny Burke and Victor van Heusen); its jokes, bland (about the camel: "Think we got enough gas?" and about the desert: "This must be where they empty all the old hourglasses!"); and its female part, underwritten. While Hope and Crosby's film allowed the stars to mug for the camera and even break the fourth wall ("But what about the people who came in the middle of the picture . . . ?," "I might win an Academy Award!"), May's makes no such concessions. *Ishtar,* in this light, reads less as an homage to the *Road* movies than as a travesty of them and of the kind of mainstream comedy that trades more on gimmicks than on good writing.

That is not to say that May's updated version is without its own flaws. A far less considered aspect of May's revision, for instance, is how much it continues to rely on caricatures of Arabic characters and culture. Its recourse to stereotype is particularly evident in the scene in which

Rogers and Clark disguise themselves as Berbers to escape detection by gunrunners, with Chuck posing as an interpreter and Lyle joining an indistinguishable group of North African tribespeople who have assembled to purchase guns from British arms dealers. The resulting exchange has Chuck lampooning North African languages and Lyle in "blue face," both cosplaying Berbers for laughs. While *Ishtar*'s treatment of the Middle East was unfortunately commonplace in contemporary blockbusters of the period, from *Raiders of the Lost Ark* (1981) to *Back to the Future* (1985), this particular gimmick—even if it is in the service of lampooning Western imperialism—understandably provoked backlash from Arab American groups.[73]

Additional criticism could have (and has) been leveled at the script's treatment of its main female character, Shira Assel, and the thinness of Adjani's part. In this case, however, one could argue that the underdevelopment is intentional—a reflection of women's afterthought status within the genre, which May retained for the sake of satire. Put differently, whether one sees the character as a missed opportunity on May's part will depend on whether one buys into the deconstructive orientation of her film with its feigned concessions to popular taste that are, in fact, not.

In a postscreening discussion at the Harvard Film Archive, May framed Hollywood's failure to capitalize on comic talent in the postwar period as a capitulation to the public: "Actually, stand-up was pretty good. It was the movies. There were some really really great stand-up guys. Carlin and Bruce and Mort Sahl. Actually in the clubs there were a lot of funny people. But somehow that didn't translate to movies, because movies were supposed to be for dumber people, you know?" (see the next section, "An Interview with Elaine May"). This comment echoes a sentiment that surfaces, somewhat improbably, in Mike Nichols's *Wolf* (1994), to whose script May is reported to have contributed. "These days, not only in corporate America but all around the globe, taste and individuality are actually something of a handicap," Christopher Plummer's publishing CEO announces to the principled editor, played by Jack Nicholson. In that film, lycanthropy ends up serving as a metaphor for nonconformity and the character's refusal to capitulate to the homogenizing forces of global capitalism. It's possible to see Rogers and Clark's outright badness, perhaps, in similarly romantic terms—as a protective idiosyncrasy that prevents their absorption into the mainstream. But it's equally possible to see *Ishtar* as a cautionary tale, not just a quixotic one, about an increasingly market-driven culture whose celebration of the mediocre has deluded even the rankest amateur into thinking that they (like America) have got talent.

Embedded in *Ishtar*'s very premise, one could say, is a swipe at the culture industry's overreliance on crowd-pleasing shtick—the proverbial "songs people know"—and distrust of what we might today refer to as original IP. By the time she made the film, May was no longer a newcomer to Hollywood but a seasoned veteran, an experienced screenwriter and script doctor for hire who had lent her talents to everything from *Reds* (1981) and *Tootsie* (1982) to *Labyrinth* (1986). Savvy as she was, it may not be too much to suggest that May invoked the *Road* movies as *her* gimmick, knowing that she would need both a "high-concept" hook and major stars to get a studio to greenlight her work in an era almost exclusively concerned with profits. In a 2008 AFI tribute to Warren Beatty, May teased her longtime collaborator for always pitching outlandish projects that sounded patently unmarketable. "When Warren is going to present a project to you that he's going to do, he manages to make it sound as crazy as possible," she said and recounted his absurdly circumlocutory pitch for *Heaven Can Wait*, followed by his description of *Reds*: "[It's] about this communist, who's this journalist, who was born in the late 1880s. . . . [H]e marries another communist, he goes back to Russia, he's the only American communist who's buried with the history . . . of whatever" ("Elaine May Salutes").[74] What she didn't say was that as a female director, lacking Beatty's industry clout, it wasn't possible for her to be quite so open about her passion projects. Instead, May worked through the crowd-pleasing plot, but with ambitions that were never straightforwardly commercial.

Ishtar, the Contrarian Text?

That *Ishtar* failed to please crowds arguably says more about studios' outsized power in determining a film's box-office fate than about May's directorial choices. But it is worth considering the heterodox elements of her approach and their potential to alienate some audiences even as those elements constitute a primary source of *Ishtar*'s appeal. As Dean Brandum has succinctly put it, "With every opportunity provided, May's instincts turned toward confounding the most popular aesthetic tropes then on display in American cinema" (148). Of course, contrarianism is a moving target and only exists in relation to the expressive norms of 1980s Hollywood, which, notably, had grown more rigid in the decade since May's filmmaking career began.

The film's casting may most clearly convey May's nonconformism. "Against type" doesn't fully describe her choice of Hoffman and Beatty for the parts of Chuck and Lyle, respectively, or account for *Ishtar*'s running metacommentary on the dissonance between the actors' off- and on-screen personae. Warren Beatty, a notorious ladies' man, plays the guy who can't get the girl, while the shorter and less conventionally attractive Hoffman is presented as a stud. When the two men walk down the street in silhouette, their height difference amplified by the goofy hunter's cap Beatty's Lyle wears, the latter bemoans his also-ran status: "You gotta have the looks, Chuck. I mean, you walk into a [bar] and the girls just want you. You know you've got that kind of face, mean-looking but with character. And the way you walk, you can only do that with a small body. You heard of a big sportscar?"

May's joke, of course, relies on the audience's knowledge of Beatty's real-life prowess and the deliberate inversion of his and Hoffman's heartthrob status. It's not merely that Beatty, in the film, plays dumb—as he had, similarly, in *Shampoo* (1975) and *Heaven Can Wait* (1978)—but that he is also, and perhaps more off-puttingly for spectators, rendered

Figure 27. *Ishtar*'s contrarianism: undercutting star persona

sexless. In this way, *Ishtar* effectively provides the opposite of fan service, forcing audiences to confront the distance between Beatty and Hoffman's fictional characters and their real-life reputations, continually referenced in the film's publicity. As *People* magazine reported, "They are Hollywood's lanky romantic Mutt and jug-sized Jeff, the lone Lothario and the big-beaked paterfamilias of the movies" (Darrach 102). *Life* magazine went so far as to shoot a cover in which Beatty basically envelops Hoffman in a bear hug, then describes them thus: "One is Hollywood, tall (six feet two), handsome and quiet. One is New York, short (five feet six), um, appealing, and brash" (Allison and Dowling 63).

Costuming extends this contrarian impulse. Both Beatty and Hoffman wear ill-fitting clothes and sport unfashionable haircuts; the lighting does neither any favors (both actors were close to fifty). Even astute critics have been stymied by May's decision to put the actors in "purposely unappealing" clothes (Brandum 143). As Brandum notes, "It would appear that the directive of the costume designer was to clothe the protagonists in the least attractive garb possible," including Isabelle Adjani, whom May kept "swathed in head scarves for most of its duration, robbing audiences (and publicity departments) of her beauty" (143). Yet such comments overlook May's clearly strategic use of costume across her filmography, first with early collaborator Anthea Sylbert and then on *Ishtar* with Anthony Powell. Here, making her celebrity actors "look bad"—or at least not like celebrities—is clearly the point.

The film's set design, especially in the New York sequences, is similarly idiosyncratic, if less immediately striking, upon a first watch of the film. Chuck's apartment, for instance, features a truly bewildering array of artifacts: magazine spreads taped to the wall, a poster of W. E. B. Du Bois, a lava lamp, a teddy bear, and an image of Simon and Garfunkel stuck behind the TV. The college dorm room aesthetic reflects Chuck's failure to launch but is never underscored; it is, again, left to the viewers to discern the meaning behind, say, his apparent fondness for kimonos and chinoiserie. Meanwhile, Lyle's home features an overstuffed couch and the detritus of his divorce-induced depression; one version of the script mentions "hot-pink curtain ties at the window and dust on the table," perfectly capturing the atmosphere of failed domesticity (28).

Finally and perhaps most significantly, there is the soundtrack. *Ishtar* may be one of the only films in history—if not *the* only film—to have produced an original score that is deliberately, if charmingly, awful. Though there was apparently an initial plan to release it, as Brandum observes, "The songs, sung off-key and purposely 'bad,' were not likely to provide a hit soundtrack album" (148). As she did in casting the film, May recruited an incomparable talent in the form of Paul Williams, only to *not* capitalize on it—which is to say, she tasked Williams with composing only believably terrible songs. If the lyrics of the film's signature tune, "Dangerous Business," have often been seen to constitute *Ishtar's* most direct swipe at the sycophancy of the studio system—"Telling the truth can be dangerous business; / Honest and popular don't go hand in hand"—it's worth considering the purposefully *unpopular* nature of the film's score as one part of May's rejoinder.

Considered cumulatively, it is hard not to conclude that May's every choice seems to have been designed to minimize the most obvious and time-tested sources of commercial appeal (catchy songs, attractive stars), which is to say, to avoid Hollywood gimmicks. To suggest that May intentionally set out to make a film ungoverned by studio priorities, however, is not to suggest she wanted it to perform poorly—May has always been open, if facetiously so, about her desire to make money. Speaking about *A New Leaf*, for instance, she told an interviewer, "I wanted to sell [the script] for a lot of money so I could be richer" (qtd. in Rivlin 81). Rather, based on the evidence of *Ishtar* and her larger body of work, it seems more accurate to suggest that May placed greater faith in the audience to recognize and reward a style of comedy less constrained by the industry's overriding mandates—distilled in the 1959 Emmy Award sketch—to make money and to "offend no one anywhere on Earth."

In *Ishtar's* final scene, Charles Grodin, representing another oppressive American regime, the CIA, has the military forcefully extract "applause" from the unwitting audience of soldiers, assembled and made to cheer for Rogers and Clark, who have cut a deal with the government to promote their album. It's a final, fitting swipe at Hollywood studios, whose methods may not seem as openly extractive but are predicated on a similar transaction: getting people's applause and, ultimately, their money. May's would-be artists are too naive to recognize the grift, but for that very reason, they're the perfect vehicles to expose it. Like Chauncy Gardener in *Being There* (1979), Chuck Clark and Lyle Rogers belong to a cinematic pantheon of accidental heroes. Much like Nichols accepting an award for "the most total mediocrity," Lyle and Clark reveal the bankruptcy of our allegedly meritocratic ideals, winning a record contract only through an absurd sequence of events and despite rather than because of their music. Through the characters' well-intentioned fumbling, *Ishtar* exposes the logic of an industry that has so thoroughly decoupled talent from success that even—or maybe only—the most singularly unqualified can triumph. Hollywood: a dangerous business, indeed.

Flopping and Feminist Film Historiography

For some fans, the lyrics to "Dangerous Business" have offered a clue to May's career downturn after *Ishtar*. After all, the song's opening lines— "Telling the truth can be dangerous business; / Honest and popular don't go hand in hand"—appear to provide a satisfying explanation for May's experience, positioning her as an uncompromising artist punished for telling unpopular "truths" in Hollywood. Yet when it comes to understanding *Ishtar*'s postrelease fate and the consequences for May's directing career, it is the closing sequence that may possess the greater explanatory power. As noted above, *Ishtar* ends with the film's hapless duo finding success of a sort, thanks not to talent or perseverance but to the interventions of the CIA, which is forced to fund the "worldwide" promotion of Rogers and Clark's album in order to prevent political turmoil in the Middle East. The scene emphasizes the compulsory nature of their "positive" reception at the Chez Casablanca. As Rogers and Clark run through their set, an army captain stalks the room, exhorting the "Seventh Battalion" members serving as seat-fillers to clap, much as a producer would elicit cheers from the audience of a talk show ("Applause! Applause! Pick it up! Applause! Yeah!").

Ishtar, in short, ends by suggesting that when it comes to art, there may be a laughably inverse relationship between popularity and quality; that the former can be engineered as much as earned; *and* that the chance of accidental success is considerably heightened when the bumblers in question are white men abetted behind the scenes by other white men. (As Jack Weston's character, Marty, says to Grodin's, "Let's work together as agents.") It's a lesson that would turn out to be all too relevant to *Ishtar*, a movie whose enduring reputation as one of the "worst films ever made"—epitomized by an infamous 1987 *Far Side* cartoon imagining "Hell's video store" as a collection of VHS copies of the film—has persisted not just *despite* the film's virtues but almost entirely independent of them. That May would choose to comment indirectly on the mercurial nature of commercial success is entirely plausible, given that by this point in her career, she had enjoyed both astronomical acclaim and its opposite. Indeed, Nichols has noted how confounding they both found the juggernaut of their own early success, especially the rapturous reception that greeted their Broadway debut. "Neither of us could understand this thing," he noted, referring to it as "the only thing we've done that was never criticized at all by anyone!" (*Mike Nichols*).

What happened to *Ishtar* is worth exploring not only because of the impact it would have on May's career but also because of its broader implications for women filmmakers. Put another way, what a so-called flop like *Ishtar* reveals is the extent to which "flopping" itself is a discursive construct as much as an empirical category and a phenomenon at once passively perpetuated—and, in May's case, actively engineered—by major studio and media outlets. As one *Slate* headline put it in a 2019 reappraisal, "*Ishtar* didn't die a natural death" (Chung). It's a sentiment echoed both by May's longtime supporters—including Nichols, who described *Ishtar*'s fate as an unparalleled instance of "studio self-sabotaging"—and by May herself, who has argued, as she did in a 2010 interview, that "the movie was *so* killed" ("Elaine May in Conversation"; Guest, postscreening discussion about *Ishtar*).

By now, May's battles with Columbia Pictures and then studio head David Puttnam have been well-documented. It's easier to underscore rather than relitigate a few of the most salient facts: that Puttnam inherited *Ishtar* after having been installed as studio chief during its production; that he had an established animus toward Beatty and Hoffman, having publicly competed and skirmished with both stars in the preceding years; and that he arrived at Columbia with a stated agenda to reform "the system" and to rein in the kind of profligate spending that he saw exemplified by *Ishtar* (Bart, "Rise"). Less established, however, has been the gendered politics of *Ishtar*'s sabotage and the flop label more generally. In this section, I consider the implications of the film's mistreatment not just for May but also for other women filmmakers in the 1970s and 1980s whose careers were curtailed, if less dramatically truncated, by metrics of success determined by a disproportionately male studio system and critical establishment.[75] By situating May's *film maudit* within the context of a broader pattern of "failure" by contemporary American women directors—including Claudia Weill, Joan Tewkesbury, and Joan Micklin Silver—it becomes clear that feminist film historians must engage not only in the recovery of female-authored texts but also in the interrogation of ideologically charged language and methods of adjudication.

The Road Back to *Ishtar*

Ishtar presents an interesting case inasmuch as its status as a flop rests not only on its box-office performance—the film is estimated to have lost approximately $41 million—but also on an openly prejudicial and a priori critical narrative that emerged prior to the film's release.[76] Even as the efforts of high-profile critics and programmers to restore its reputation have resulted in increasingly widespread appreciation for the film, the "hate-buzz" remains oddly tenacious (Heller-Nicholas 5). On Twitter, for instance, *Ishtar* continues to be invoked as a lazy punch line. As recently as 2020, blue-checkmark screenwriter and author Rex Pickett responded to a pro-*Ishtar* tweet from former *New York Times* film critic Janet Maslin in several since-deleted posts by first asserting his disdain for the film, which he called a "dinosaur turd" and a "meme of cinematic failure," and then attacking the young (female) journalist who came to its defense: "How dare you disallow me to have an opinion in a profession I've spent my whole life in. Bitch!"[77] In so doing, he put on full display the kind of reactionary sexism that has arguably played a role in shaping critical response to the film since before its release.

This exchange reflects the deeply held belief in May's incompetence and the staying power of a narrative that began to attach itself to her at least a decade earlier, during the production of *Mikey and Nicky* (1976). As critics have noted, the narrative of May's "unruliness" was linked to May's allegedly profligate waste of both money and celluloid during the *Mikey and Nicky* shoot (Heller-Nicholas 5). In fact, this perception dates back to her very first foray into directing. In his memoirs, for instance, former Paramount executive Peter Bart recalls his immediate distaste at the prospect of working on *A New Leaf* (*Infamous Players* 145). Describing May as "an individual who is not only unprepared but indifferent to mastering the intricacies of filmmaking," Bart offers a series of prejudicial allegations, portraying her as irrational ("it seemed all but impossible to reason with her") and indecisive ("[she] constantly changed her mind about the actors' lines and the camera angle" [146]). When the studio ultimately decided to hire an editor to shorten May's original three-hour cut, Bart excused their extreme course of action by admitting it was not one "we would follow with a respected filmmaker, but none of us respected Elaine May" (147).

This somewhat incoherent construction of May—as at once inept and uncompromising, imprudent and principled—would return with a vengeance in the coverage of the higher-profile *Ishtar* and achieve mythic status in a May 1987 cover story David Blum wrote about its production for *New York* magazine. The piece featured a series of unflattering anecdotes, including an infamous story about May's "alleged search for the perfect camel," most of which were attributed to anonymous "production sources" or Columbia "staffers." Blum emphasized her extravagance throughout, reporting that "Elaine May ended up shooting more than 50 takes of one scene, with three cameras rolling at all times." Twenty years later, Peter Biskind would continue this characterization, writing in a dishy piece excerpted from his biography of Beatty about the chaotic "madness" of the *Ishtar* shoot.

What makes the discourse of May's "madness" especially galling, however, is that many of the behaviors that Blum, Biskind, and others singled out for caricature—May's perfectionism, her "control freak tendencies," her obsessive dedication to her craft at whatever cost— are of course the very qualities historically celebrated when associated with and embodied by any number of exacting male directors. As Manohla Dargis put it, Blum's anecdotes seem designed to suggest that "May—unlike, say, your favorite male auteur—was an *unreasonable* perfectionist." It is just one example of the way auteurism was mobilized against May in press coverage. Or, as director Claudia Weill has put it in a more recent interview, "If you shot more than three takes as a woman, it was like, Oh, my gosh, she doesn't know what she's doing. But if Michael Cimino did 190 takes, he was a genius!" (Press).

Indeed, just a few years earlier, Beatty himself, while shooting *Reds*—another high-profile production with a lavish budget, A-list cast, and challenging location shoots—was reportedly engaged in practices nearly identical to May's. As Biskind writes, this time of Beatty's direction, he "wouldn't stop the camera . . . [doing] it all in one run until the roll of film ran out," and he insisted on a large number of takes, as many as seventy or eighty by some accounts ("Thunder").[78] In this case, however, such anecdotes were offered as proof of Beatty's heroic devotion to a cinematic cause rather than as evidence of fumbling. "Beatty shot an impressive number of takes," Biskind wrote in a retrospective appreciation of the film, "Thunder on the Left: The Making of *Reds*," which is as adulatory as his piece on *Ishtar* was critical. He added approvingly that "[Beatty] generally liked to give himself lots of choices in the editing room, and always thought that the best take was just around the corner." Yet May, doing much the same, was apparently just burning celluloid. In short, while May was "making a $40 million farce in the desert" (Blum), Beatty was "defy[ing] Hollywood wisdom by making . . . a big-budget docudrama . . . a stunning epic about American communists" (Biskind, "Thunder"). May's "madness" becomes Beatty's "thunder."

Similarly off-putting to many contemporary critics was the belief that May had wasted not just funding or film stock but also, effectively, her leading men, reflected in the oddly breathless pull quote in Blum's article, that "May had decided to play two stars against their public persona." Indeed, there has been surprising consensus that "aside from its notorious production history, the problem with *Ishtar* wasn't that it was necessarily a 'bad' film, but that it cast Beatty and Hoffman . . . in roles so dramatically against type" (Heller-Nicholas 5). Yet similarly counterintuitive casting wasn't held against male collaborators such as Beatty and Nichols. Writing of *Reds*, for instance, Roger Ebert noted that both Beatty and Diane Keaton were "a tad unlikely as casting choices" yet went on to praise their performances, citing Keaton's as "a particular surprise" and allowing that, even if she was better known for playing "touchy New Yorker[s]," here she was "just what she need[ed] to be." Mike Nichols's choice of Hoffman for the lead in *The Graduate*, meanwhile, was seen as ingenious rather than eccentric, with *Life* magazine, for one, congratulating Nichols for giving "homely non-hero Dustin Hoffman an unlikely role in *The Graduate*" (Zeitlin). The problem for many reviewers, then, may not have been the unlikeliness of May's casting so much as the perceived audaciousness of her decision to downgrade two of Hollywood's leading men, in the language of the film, to schmucks.

Ultimately, however, it was the relentless focus on *Ishtar*'s budget that may best reflect the critical double standards at work. There's no doubt, of course, that *Ishtar* was a costly production—though May, in a 2010 interview with Haden Guest, flatly contested the budget numbers released by the studio, which put the budget at nearly $50 million, and agreed when he pointed out that "Hollywood has a long history of releasing dummy figures" (postscreening discussion about *Ishtar*). Regardless, the numbers were not sufficient to explain the extent to which, in Richard Brody's words, "what dominated news reports in the months prior to [*Ishtar*'s] release—and . . . what most critics seemed to review—was the budget rather than the movie" ("Elaine"). As Charles Grodin has repeatedly observed, the concern with the film's financials was irrational bordering on obsessive: "It actually became part of the title. You always saw it referenced as 'the $50 million *Ishtar*.' . . . Why should the public be concerned what the budget of a movie is?" After all, he added, it wasn't as if Columbia "was going to give the money to the people of America rather than spend it" (qtd. in Bennett). However, if, as Robin Wood argued in an essay published one year before *Ishtar*'s release, the real "aversion is to women's power made visible and concrete," the public fixation on budget as a signifier of female ambition begins to make more sense (186).

In fact, the financial data that have often been furnished as objective "proof" of *Ishtar*'s failure take on a different cast when considered in historical context. It's especially instructive to compare May's outing at the box office with two later films Beatty would go on to make, *Town and Country* (2001) and *Rules Don't Apply* (2016), which, as Chad Perman has pointed out, "ended up losing far more money than *Ishtar* ever did." Meanwhile, Nichols's 1975 film, *The Fortune*, which also starred Beatty as one half of a hapless duo, was deemed both a critical and commercial failure, but in his case the disaster proved survivable and would be eclipsed by his subsequent filmography. (Two other ultimately inconsequential misfires for Nichols are *Catch-22* [1970], his sophomore effort, and *Wolf* [1994].) Indeed, we could point to any number of other films whose poor showings had comparatively little impact on their directors' careers. May, by contrast, would never direct another feature film after *Ishtar*. While the Wikipedia list of "biggest box-office bombs" may be a blunt instrument, even a glance at it attests to the wildly unequal distribution of both opportunity and room for error among male and female directors. In 1978 the *New York Times* ran a story headlined "Women Film Directors: Will They, Too, Be Allowed to Bomb?" (Honeycutt). Based on the evidence, both empirical and anecdotal, the answer to this question not just then but forty-five years later still seems to be an emphatic "no."

It is true, of course, that it was not only women directors like May who would experience the negative repercussions of the blockbuster era, in which, as Tom Shone notes, "even the failures [were] events" (211). With *Heaven's Gate*, for instance, Michael Cimino found himself, like May, up against "a force field of inverse glamour so great . . . it obscured the actual movie just as surely as any amount of hype" (211). If this outsized reaction was, as Shone argues, "a direct, antibody response to the amount of hoopla pumped into the public bloodstream," it was also an indicator of just how easily popular reaction and box-office performance could be rigged (211). In this light, it feels disingenuous to insist that "flopping" is exclusively a numbers game or that, as a phenomenon, it is equally survivable—or critically disinterested. Instead, *Ishtar*'s fate suggests that the term "flop" can be less descriptive than proscriptive and that its very invocation should be understood, at least in certain contexts, to constitute a powerful form of gatekeeping.

"Industrial Lore" and Hollywood's Logics of Exclusion

If *Ishtar* serves as a cautionary tale, then, what it cautions against is not the excess of individual directors so much as the illiberalism of studios, which amid women's increased activism during the 1970s continued to enforce "the conditions under which women [were] permitted to make films" (Wood 186).[79] May's experience reveals just how narrow those conditions were and how constrained even an established and comparatively powerful figure would have been by the industry's entrenched assumptions about gender, genre, and the "bankability" of women directors.[80] As Rebecca Sheehan has put it, summing up the general sentiment at the time, there were "institutionalised beliefs that women were innately incapable of and so could not be trusted with the financial, technical, and creative aspects of filmmaking" (2).

Risk aversion would have been a particular concern at the moment May was shooting *Ishtar* in the mid-1980s. Gone were the (comparatively) freewheeling days of New Hollywood, with its (selective) enthusiasm for visionary auteurs. If already in the 1970s the "prevalent discourse about women . . . was that they lacked the creative breadth, technical mastery, financial sense, business acumen, and ability to command respect that were critical for directing," then the heightening of the economic stakes in the 1980s no doubt did little to help the case of women directors confronting a "gendered logic of risk" that persists to this day (Sheehan 7; Donoghue 8).

Genre also presented another avenue for exclusion. While making *Mikey and Nicky*, May had already felt saddled by the expectation that she produce a comedy. Now she experienced a different variety of pigeonholing. Those around her—including cast and crew members—voiced concerns that she was not "up to" the task of shooting action. Biskind's account of the *Ishtar* shoot, for instance, quotes Paul Sylbert saying that May lacked the expertise needed for the final shoot-out: "She knew nothing about action sequences. A battle scene for this woman who had done everything in improvisation? You can't improvise a battle scene" (*Star* 355). These comments are consistent with a historical pattern of discrimination that continues in contemporary Hollywood and that has frequently seen women directors consigned to the "pink ghetto" of comedy—especially romantic and teen comedy—and "shut out of big budget genres like action, science fiction, and comic book movies" (Donoghue 2). In the case of her last two films, especially, May seems to have been almost preemptively punished for not staying in her lane and, with *Ishtar*, for having the presumption to attempt a film that would take a sizable amount of money to produce. Even today, Courtney Brannon Donoghue notes, "a narrative persists that women as a group lack the experience to helm big-budget projects" (5).

Finally, there's the brute fact of May's gender in an industry in which the "category of director" was—and arguably still is—"masculinized" (Sheehan 3). Sheehan suggests that women in 1970s Hollywood existed in "conceptual quarantine from the discourse of profitable, relatable, and creative authorship"—a prospect certainly borne out by the experiences of contemporaries such as production designer Polly Platt, whose definitive contributions to then husband Peter Bogdanovich's earliest films were until recently largely omitted from the historical record (3).[81] Moreover, when women did beat the odds, as May would, they inevitably faced both outsized expectations and excessive oversight. "As exceptions in a male-dominated industry," Sheehan notes, "women directors' work methods and output were subject to intense scrutiny by their crews, by film studio executives and employees, and by journalists reporting about them" (2). May's career provides particularly damning evidence of this trend, given how many crew members have been willing to go on the record with unflattering anecdotes and how readily this generally anonymized testimony has been granted credence. Biskind's reporting on *Ishtar*, for instance, makes frequent use of unreliable testimony. As associate editor Billy Scharf noted, Paul Sylbert—one of May's most vocal critics—was clearly biased: "[He] hated her" (qtd. in Biskind, *Star* 349). The impossibly high stakes didn't help. For instance, Todd McCarthy, May's assistant on *Mikey and Nicky*, publicly blamed May not only for the production's difficulties but also for no less than "set[ting] back the cause of women directors in Hollywood by ten years" (qtd. in Smukler, *Liberating Hollywood* 92).

In hindsight, then, it seems clear that *Ishtar*'s fate was not just predetermined but also overdetermined, its "failure" all but guaranteed by studios upholding a certain set of economic logics and invested in frankly sexist industry lore. Cognizant as May surely was of the stacked odds, she has rarely acknowledged the double standards she confronted in any but the most elliptical terms. For instance, in a piece of faux publicity for the 1990 film *In the Spirit*, May allowed herself to be interviewed by costar Marlo Thomas, who asked her point-blank: "How do you feel about being a writer and a director in what is predominantly a white-male-dominated world?" In response, May offered a series of deflections:

ELAINE: You mean . . . is it fun?
MARLO: No, forget fun. We're off fun. I mean, most of the executives, directors and screenwriters in Hollywood are men. So how do you feel about being in what is mostly a men's club?
ELAINE: Can we turn off the tape for a minute?
MARLO: No. Bella Abzug once said, "Real equality is going to come not when a female Einstein is recognized as quickly as a male Einstein but when a female schlemiel is promoted as quickly as a male schlemiel." What's your feeling about that?
ELAINE: Well, I think there are probably more female schlemiels in high positions now than when I started, although it's true that there

are no female schlemiels in the highest position. But I think that, in time, there will be.

MARLO: That's not the point I'm making. (*Growing Up Laughing* 333–34)

One way of interpreting May's ironic engagement with this question is that the answer is so obvious that it need not be supplied. How else is one *supposed* to feel about the industry's entrenched sexism? No increase in female executives, May's answer implies, will change the rules of the game. If she has avoided discussing her experience of Hollywood bias, there is no doubt she lived it, having encountered the full range of preconceptions about women—that they "lacked the creative breadth, technical mastery, financial sense, business acumen, and ability to command respect that were critical for directing"—over the course of her filmmaking career (Sheehan 7).

It's *Not* Your Turn

If May was made vulnerable by the scale of her ambitions—afflicted by what one writer has called the "Curse of Bigness"—it is worth acknowledging the women filmmakers of the 1970s and 1980s who were seemingly penalized for the inverse transgression: making films not big or broadly appealing *enough* (Raban 193). Though smaller budgets and more modestly scaled ambitions mitigate the risks of flopping per se, they also maximize the likelihood a film might "fail" in different ways: to find its audience, to make money, to gain visibility, or to win awards. It seems hardly incidental, after all, that women directors as talented and diverse as Joan Micklin Silver, Claudia Weill, Jane Wagner, Joan Darling, and Joan Tewkesbury, among others, not to mention Black women directors such as Julie Dash, often managed to make no more than one or two films before transitioning into made-for-TV movies or episodic television direction. Meanwhile, even commercially successful contemporaries such as Amy Heckerling and Susan Seidelman would eventually find their filmmaking careers limited or prematurely abridged. There's a particular irony in considering that the title of Weill's 1980 film, a follow-up to her celebrated 1978 debut *Girlfriends*, was *It's My Turn*. As it happened, it would be the last feature she ever directed.

The difficulties have been especially acute for the group Christina Lane calls "commercially minded feminist media-makers," women directors who have elected to work in more mainstream genres and channels (72). Writing of Seidelman's 2013 film *The Hot Flashes*, which like much of her late career work was creatively financed and distributed, Lane notes the tension between the specific material conditions of women's filmmaking and the ahistorical conceptions of success to which they are subjected: "[*The Hot Flashes*] can be held up . . . as a model of feminist entrepreneurialism and savvy. Yet, in the unsettled environment where indie features intersect with emergent media trends, there is no effective way to tabulate its proceeds outside the theatrical box office figures, which comprise the least of its profits" (81). In short, Lane asks, "In the midst of so much change . . . *what counts as success?*" (81, italics mine). It's a question that has not been sufficiently interrogated, as the case of *Ishtar* reveals, and the answer remains, arguably, too reflexively determined by a self-appointed and disproportionately male body of arbiters, many of them gatekeepers of major studios or media outlets. In fact, what Lane's analysis of Seidelman's career underscores is the vital importance of defining "success" within a greater attention to the contexts in which women's filmmaking has occurred and the urgency of such definitional work to the project of feminist media history.

In this spirit, it's worth considering the revised framework proposed by Jane Gaines in response to the "disappearance" of women from the silent film historical record:

> It is tempting to say, in answer to the intellectual history "what happened" question, that [women] were "forgotten" by later critics. But here the language of forgetting implies memory lapse or benign neglect, and thus erases the struggle over inclusion and exclusion. A more political approach might think in terms of knowledge apportionment, a rationing of the women credited in the industry story of triumphant corporatization. Or, this is the case of what could be called the *unequal distribution of narrative wealth*, a relegation of a larger portion of credit to men to which women demurred. (22)

Inspired by Gaines, we could also think in terms of *success* apportionment as a way of understanding the highly "unequal distribution" of prestige and acclaim. Only by calling out, for instance, the deliberate, purposeful "rationing of women" in critical canons can we disrupt the mystifying discussions of the "spectral" Elaine May, which take for granted the marginalization of May or her female peers, and redress the causes of their disappearance. Put another way, it is not enough simply to recover exceptional work by women; instead, we have to reckon with default evaluative structures and nomenclature—"guilty pleasure," "chick flick"—that have contributed to women's exclusion in the first place.

In so doing, critics and scholars must also confront the limits of "recovery" as a theoretical framework, as Alix Beeston advocates in her discussion of the unfinished films of American playwright and filmmaker Kathleen Collins. Calling it an "overdetermining frame . . . in the contemporary global markets for women's film, literature, and art," Beeston describes the troubling ubiquity of this logic: "It's as if virtually every woman artist and author in history is now available to us as a discovery: she who once was lost is now found by a culture that claims itself redemptive, even heroic, in the gesture" (246, 247). If May herself was never quite "lost" in the way a director like Collins was, she has been subjected to—and, indeed, is currently experiencing—a valedictory, late-career reappreciation following a period of critical neglect, during which her films were out of circulation and difficult to find. The arc of May's own career, in fact, is not dissimilar to the one that continues to be experienced by female filmmakers. As Donoghue writes, "Hollywood routinely discovers and rediscovers the box office weight of women. Looking back over trade coverage since the 2000s, a pattern of recognition, celebration, and forgetting emerges" (11). In May's case, this cycle has also featured critical outrage, to be sure. But the pattern is additionally, and importantly, complicated by May's own decisive interventions and the considerable work that she has continued to do—as a screenwriter and actor—subsequent to her directorial career and without evident concern for critical consensus or recognition. May, in short, doesn't need anyone's recovery.

Coda: May's New Leaf?

In 2016 May completed a documentary about Mike Nichols's career for the *American Masters* series, her only directing credit since *Ishtar*.

(Much of the footage, including original interviews, was completed before Nichols died in 2014.) As an hour-long profile originally broadcast on PBS, the documentary is in a category different from May's features, but it nonetheless bears some of her cinematic trademarks. It begins, for instance, with Mozart's *Eine kleine Nachtmusik* playing over the title card before a hard cut to newsreel footage of Hitler—hardly the expected opening for a genre that tends toward the bland and hagiographic. "I was born in Berlin," Nichols begins, and while the footage of *der Führer* is certainly functional—setting up Nichols's recollection of his family's escape from Nazi Germany—it is also a little bit cheeky.

It's one example of the way May has managed to make her signature felt across the wide range of projects she has contributed to during the more than two decades since *Ishtar*'s release. As discussed in the introduction, May has during these years consolidated her reputation as one of the industry's premier screenwriters and script doctors, winning an Oscar nomination for the *Primary Colors* screenplay, at the same time that she has pursued various roles for both the stage and the big and small screen. (In 2021, for instance, she unexpectedly appeared in the pandemic-era film *The Same Storm*, directed by Peter Hedges, in which she steals every one of the Zoom-chat-recorded scenes she's in.) In short, she has been consistently active and creatively productive even as she has maintained a relatively low public profile—until recently. In 2019 May's acclaimed performance as Gladys in the Broadway revival of *The Waverly Gallery* earned her a Tony Award and a renewed level of visibility. Shortly after, rumors surfaced that she would be directing a film called *Crackpot*, starring Dakota Johnson.[82] While that speculation remains unsubstantiated by May herself, the excitement that greeted the news hinted at May's growing popularity with newer audiences.

Figure 28. Recent appearances: *The Same Storm* (2021)

Indeed, even as she has been the recipient of major awards in recent years—a Tony, an honorary Oscar, the National Medal of Arts—she has received broader recognition in popular culture, appearing as Ruth Bader Ginsburg on an episode of *The Good Fight* and serving as an obvious source of inspiration for the hit series *The Marvelous Mrs. Maisel* (2017–23). The excitement that greeted the show, which is about a young and attractive Jewish female comedian who is explicitly *not* Elaine May but who will repeatedly invoke her as an influence, speaks to May's contemporary resonance. At the same time, the series allowed itself the present-day privilege of commenting on the conditions that historically jeopardized the success of comedians such as May. When, in the show's pilot, protagonist Midge Maisel launches into a set skewering her ex-husband and the failures of men more generally, a heckler calls out, "Women aren't funny," and then, a minute later, "dumb bitch."

Presuming May's popularity continues to grow, it will not be a coincidence or an inevitability. Rather, it will reflect the fact that history finally appears to be catching up to May as both an artist and a keen social observer who offered prescient dispatches about our culture's dysfunctional status quo before filmgoers were necessarily ready to hear them. Indeed, as an artist who has always worked across media, May might actually be more legible to contemporary audiences for whom

Figure 29. *The Marvelous Mrs. Maisel*: An homage to May (and Nichols)

multihyphenate creators have increasingly become the norm. For me, then, May ultimately belongs not only to film history but also to a broader genealogy of women writers, from Gertrude Stein and Virginia Woolf to Joan Didion, who are as unwavering and clear-eyed in their critiques as they are precise and idiosyncratic in their prose. All three issued coolly detached pronouncements about the historical moments in which they found themselves and clocked their respective "lost generations." May arguably worked in this dispassionate tradition, well aware that devastating truths are often best delivered casually in the context of a story or joke that might appear to be about something else. Watch the "Water Cooler" skit today, and the line that hits likely isn't about the exposure of Charles Van Doren as a fraud ("He was my idol!") or the phoniness of politicians who don't write their own speeches. Instead, it's the moment when May's character, applauding the government's swift response to another quiz-show scandal, observes, "Well, they can't fool around with this the way they did with integration!" What drew a laugh from the television audience in 1960 might today elicit surprise at just how deftly May delivers this searing assessment of the country's seemingly endless capacity for dithering when it comes to real social change. As the kids might say: *I'm dead.*

In the *American Masters* documentary, Nichols shares an anecdote that may indirectly speak to May's genius for truth-telling. Reflecting on his mediocre career as a University of Chicago student, Nichols recalls one professor, Ned Rosenbaum, who called him out, recognizing that he had been coasting on charm. As Nichols put it, "He saw through me and it made a change." Although this anecdote is not about May, it's not difficult to conclude that she did something similar for Nichols. His relationship with May, after all, began with a moment of brutal honesty, when May expressed disdain for the apparently very bad Strindberg production in which Nichols appeared: "I knew she knew it was shit, and there was no way I could let her know that I knew it also" (qtd. in Harris 33). In short, she saw through his pretenses much as she saw through, basically, everyone's. There's a knowingness that blazes forth from even the seemingly lightest of May's films, a glance that misses nothing, that lets no one off the hook but that also doesn't say we can't laugh about it. If a new generation turns to her films, it will be because they help us to see, too: because May teaches us how to look.

Notes

The majority of quotations from films included throughout the text are transcribed directly from the films. When these quotations are copied from a screenplay, I've indicated as much and added page numbers.

1. Rebecca Sheehan identifies five women who directed films for major studios during the 1970s: Joan Darling, Jane Wagner, Joan Micklin Silver, Lina Wertmüller, and May (1–2). May was also just the third woman to be inducted into the Directors Guild of America, after Dorothy Arzner and Ida Lupino, in 1969.

2. The reference here is to Peter Biskind's popular history of the New Hollywood period, *Easy Riders, Raging Bulls* (1998), which helped to codify many of the "myths" of the era.

3. Having denied May the freedom to select her own director, Paramount countered by offering her the chance to direct *A New Leaf* herself. This is how, according to May, she ended up directing, writing, and starring in the film for $50,000, less than what Walter Matthau was paid for his performance alone. See Probst 129–30.

4. In the notes for the program J. Hoberman cocurated on "Hollywood's 'Jew Wave'" at Lincoln Center in 2011, he describes this moment as one in which mainstream cinema "featured a hitherto unspeakable degree of Jewish content."

5. See Nicholas Godfrey's recent study (2018) of the "limits" of conventional auteurism for film historiography. Recent volumes, including *When the Movies Mattered: The New Hollywood Revisited*, edited by Jonathan Kirshner and Jon Lewis (2019) and *The Other Hollywood Renaissance*, edited by Dominic Lennard, R. Barton Palmer, and Murray Pomerance (2022), are framed as revisionist but largely consider the same canon of films and retain a focus on male directors.

6. This phrase appeared as part of a longer tweet by *New Yorker* critic Richard Brody, who wrote on April 21, 2019, "Happy birthday to Elaine May, studio victim; all of her films are great, each in its own way—but *Mikey and Nicky* is a leap ahead of the first two in style and composition; it should have opened new paths, in her career and in the cinema at large; instead, the gates slammed shut."

7. Carrie Courogen's biography, *Miss May Does Not Exist: The Life and Work of Elaine May, Hollywood's Hidden Genius*, is scheduled for publication by Macmillan in June 2024.

8. May's exact comment was, "This is a very emotional night for me because 10, 20, 30 years ago tonight I bought this dress. . . . I bought it for Mike's first lifetime achievement award" ("Elaine May Salutes").

9. As Nora Ephron notes, writing of her own "failure," *Heartburn*, some "flops eventually bec[o]me cult hits, which is your last and final hope for a flop" (106–7).

10. The phrase "May Renaissance" appeared in a blurb that critic Ian Mantgani provided for the Edinburgh University Press's volume on May's career. Actor Natasha Lyonne and *New Yorker* writer Rachel Syme are among those who have repeatedly championed (and defended) May's work on Twitter.

11. See Godfrey for a critical account of the New Hollywood period's reliance on auteurist assessment and its implications for women directors.

12. Nichols himself has publicly dismissed the auteur theory as a "froggy conspiracy"—a reference to the *Cahiers du cinéma* critics who advanced the *politique des auteurs*—even as he conceded that decisions on a given film should come "from one mind" (*Mike Nichols*).

13. See Smukler, *Liberating Hollywood*, for an account of May's engagement (or lack thereof) with second-wave feminism.

14. It's an assessment that represents almost a complete reversal of Haskell's earlier criticisms of May. In a scathingly negative review of *Mikey and Nicky*, for instance, she accuses May of technical incompetence ("May hasn't come any closer to mastering the basics of filmmaking or developing a feel for the medium" ["Long Day's Journey" 37]) and unjustified egoism. She concludes by excoriating the "misogyny that binds [May] to her male characters and is so casually contemptuous of the females" (37).

15. See Rebecca Sheehan for a historical account of the ways the few women directing studio films during the decade were made to bear these outsized expectations.

16. According to Martha M. Lauzen's annual Celluloid Ceiling report, which has been tracking women's behind-the-scenes employment in Hollywood since 2000, the number of women working as directors on the 250 top-grossing films is back to the all-time "high" of 18 percent in 2022 after a percentage point dip to 17 percent in 2021.

17. Joe McElhaney is one of the few to note that the details "are incomplete and contradictory."

18. Julian Schlossberg, interview by the author, November 17, 2022.

19. Claudio Getti's reporting for *Il sole 24 ore*, which appeared in the *New York Review of Books*, put forward a claim about Ferrante's identity despite her stated desire for privacy.

20. This quote is taken from Michael Rivlin's account of May's reply to an interview with Leonard Probst, who himself published a somewhat divergent account of the same exchange. In Probst's telling, May responds to the question, "Why do you hide?" more vaguely by answering, "Oh, I don't know" (129).

21. Even sympathetic accounts of May tend to present her through the sexualized gaze of male collaborators. In a biography of Warren Beatty, for instance, the writer included an excerpt from a letter that notes offhandedly that "Warren is only interested in women he can have sex with, except for Pauline Kael and Elaine May" (Amburn 104).

22. See Courtney Brannon Donoghue for a discussion of "industry lore," a term she borrows from Tim Havens to describe the gendered repercussions of conventional industry wisdom for women filmmakers.

23. At another point, he confirmed that "I nagged the hell out of her. I was always saying, 'You're taking too long over this'" (qtd. in Nachman 349).

24. See McElhaney for a detailed reading of Lila's dissident temporality in that film.

25. See Stevens, "Tossing Truths," and especially Nachman's *Seriously Funny* for a detailed account of Nichols and May's enduring influence on comedy (319–59).

26. For a detailed discussion of the forms of improvisation that took place on *The Heartbreak Kid*, Simon's frustrated reaction, and the decision by producer Michael Hausman to overlook the resulting deviations from the script, see Wasson 158–60.

27. Elsewhere, Nichols has also attributed to May another dictum, that "everything they did together should be a fight, a negotiation, or a seduction," and credits her with the wisdom, "when in doubt, seduce" (qtd. in Harris 59).

28. Gerald Nachman, in his history of postwar American comedy, echoes this idea, calling May an "endlessly noodling actor-writer" (compared to Nichols's more commercially minded "director") (337).

29. Janet Coleman, for instance, notes that Compass Players colleague David Shepherd has shared his first memory of May, carrying "a raggedy manuscript of a play she was writing called *Mikey and Nicky*" (65).

30. Lauren Berlant's concept of cruel optimism is a generative one for thinking about May's films; in many ways, her work dramatized the operations of the phenomenon years before Berlant would define them.

31. This line is from Jean Renoir's 1939 film, *The Rules of the Game*, spoken by the character Octave, played by Renoir himself.

32. Apparently, Didion had the idea of starting a cooperative of script doctors, but it never got off the ground (Malone).

33. See Sam Wasson for an account of Elaine May's contributions to the *Ghostbusters II* script. "Rather than ply [the writers] with suggestions," he notes, "May offered specific, often mundane, story question. . . . A week later, [Harold] Ramis found himself on surer ground. 'It made it all clear,' he said, 'at least in our own minds'" (308).

34. See Wasson for more discussion of May's work on *Tootsie*, which Nichols called "Elaine's most spectacular save" (264–65).

35. Julian Schlossberg has denied that May played any role in directing *In the Spirit*. However, May did create a delightful mock trailer for the film, in which the cast pretends to attack Schlossberg as the film's producer. The trailer is available on YouTube.

36. It is worth noting that both of May's collaborations with Allen predate Dylan Farrow's renewed accusations against her stepfather in 2017, if only because their work together took place at a moment before the public outcry that greeted actors who subsequently chose to appear in Allen's films.

37. Edmund Wilson offers the almost identical comment: "She transforms herself so completely in her various roles that until I saw her off the stage I had no real idea how she looked" (36).

38. Schlossberg in conversation with Elaine May, Oct. 10, 2023, 92NY, New York.

39. According to her friend and collaborator Julian Schlossberg, Cary Grant read the script and was interested in the part of Henry but balked at the swimming that would be required in the final sequence. May turned him down because, as she said, "I knew nothing then. I didn't even know about doubles or stand-ins" (*Try* 290–91).

40. See Dyer for an account of the way aspects of mise-en-scène, performance, and casting might register "resistance" to genre conventions.

41. In her discussion of dialogue in screwball comedy, Sarah Kozloff highlights the importance of the verbal "match" between the romantic leads: "In screwballs we are supposed to notice, not only that the central couple are uniquely suited for each other by the way their talk is synchronized, but also that other potential suitors . . . are all wrong" (174).

42. Vincent Canby's original review of the films in the *New York Times* and Samm Deighan's essay in the recent Edinburgh University Press volume on May's work are good examples of this critical tendency.

43. See, for instance, J. Hoberman's comment that "*The Heartbreak Kid* was widely seen as an answer to *The Graduate*, directed as it was by Mike Nichols's former standup partner" ("Flaunting It"). Similarly, Vince Canby's original review notes that "Charles Grodin inevitably recalls Dustin Hoffman in *The Graduate*."

44. As McElhaney notes, "The visual and dramatic rhetoric of the films repeatedly situates the spectator's own look at these often painful and embarrassing situations as another type of witnessing, the spectator helpless to do anything aside from laugh—and sometimes not even that."

45. See Smukler (*Liberating Hollywood*, 86) for an overview of the film's negative reception among feminist critics.

46. Interestingly, Fassbinder's *Martha* (1974)—a domestic melodrama that is also an excoriating portrait of a marriage—appears to allude to *The Heartbreak Kid* by featuring a scene in which the sadistic husband allows his new bride to get horribly sunburned.

47. As McElhaney points out, "In neither Simon's screenplay nor in the Friedman story on which that screenplay was based is Lila Jewish. May's insistence on this point transforms *The Heartbreak Kid* into a different kind of project."

48. As J. Hoberman wrote in the *New York Times*, "Seemingly improvised by two method actors, *Mickey and Nicky* was totally scripted" ("In *Mikey and Nicky*"). May's longtime collaborator and *Mikey and Nicky* distributor Julian Schlossberg corroborated this account, as did Jonathan Rosenbaum, who, after reading the *Mikey and Nicky* shooting script, "discovered that the improvisational feel of the film was attributable only to the success of May and her actors in conveying her powerful writing."

49. See Berliner for an account of "narrative incoherence" in the context of 1970s American filmmaking.

50. For instance, in his recently published memoir, Schlossberg, distributor of *Mikey and Nicky* and May's frequent collaborator, described the process of working with her: "It is a joy. It is a challenge. It is the most stimulating, the most exciting experience you can have. And yet . . . " (236).

51. See Carr for an account of the continuities in approach.

52. Molly Haskell, for one, wrote a review for the *Village Voice* that basically framed it as a Cassavetes film: "A pretext for Falk and Cassavetes to indulge in one of those long, lugubrious Actors' Studio exercises that wore out its welcome with the last frame of *Husbands* and the first frame of *The Killing of a Chinese Bookie*" ("Long Day's Journey" 37).

53. As Carr points out, *Mikey and Nicky* shows Peter Falk's character ministering to a male friend rather than a neurotic wife, as he had done in Cassavetes's *A Woman under the Influence*, completed the year May began shooting (123). In place of Nick and Mabel, then, May focuses on Nick and Mikey.

54. As Schlossberg comments, "There's nothing glamorous about *Mikey and Nicky*. . . . [I]t's not *The Godfather*" ("Commentary").

55. Quart sees *Mikey and Nicky* as "the ultimate statement on a series of male buddy films that greeted the rise of feminism in the 1970s" (44).

56. Brad Stevens ("Male Narrative"), for one, notes the film's success in making explicit the queer subtext of 1970s buddy cinema, in which the woman becomes the medium through which men express their repressed longing for each other.

57. See Canford 64–66 for an account of Mayor Rizzo's meeting with the cast and crew.

58. Canford quotes production assistant Jackie Peters as suggesting that the two did help shape the script: "They put *some* things in. They got together and rehearsed long before any of us ever saw a shooting script" (81).

59. See Barthes for a fuller articulation of the difference between the "readerly" and "writerly" text, the latter of which "make[s] the reader no longer a consumer, but a producer of the text" (4).

60. Peter Cooper, in a book-length appreciation of the film that also draws on original interviews with producer Michael Hausman, quotes actor Joyce Van Patton as saying, "It was her understanding that May was 'writing about her relatives'" (7, and see 7–9 for more on the film's biographical origins). See also publicist Tom Miller's chapter on the film. In it, he recounts a conversation with May's cousin and *Mikey and Nicky* production assistant Jackie Peters, in which she confirmed that "the germ of *Mikey and Nicky* originated in [their] uncle's story. . . . [S]omething that had happened in the early stages of the Second World War, or just previous to it" (Canford 60).

61. The quotation is attributed by Miller to Scoppa when he was asked to provide a rationale for May's detailed attention to props and set design.

62. "Yes, we cast the head of Paramount, Frank Yablans, in Ned Beatty's part, and he was fantastic. He would drive up. We were rehearsing, I forget where, he would drive up in his limo and get out and then join the cast and rehearse.

And the real owner of Paramount, a man named Charles Bluhdorn, called him and said, 'What are you doing? You're the head of Paramount, you're playing a killer in a movie? And it's a small part?' So he quit" (see the next section, "An Interview with Elaine May"). Publicist Tom Miller reports that before casting Ned Beatty, May offered the part to Bob Fosse, but there is no evidence to corroborate this suggestion (Canford 82).

63. The story has acquired almost mythic status and remains unconfirmed by May, who has only said somewhat obliquely that "someone stole the negative" (see the next section, "An Interview with Elaine May").

64. A point that Nichols himself makes in the interview, noting the film's prescience and that it "invented the perfect metaphor for the behavior of the Bush administration in Iraq" ("Elaine May in Conversation").

65. Dean Brandum, for one, has described *Ishtar* as a "tract on American unexceptionalism" (151).

66. See Wyatt for a detailed account of this shift.

67. Once again, *Ishtar* created what McElhaney calls a "complex structure of looking," so that even if May's films center male characters in the narrative, "the characters' status as *schmucks* places this 'male gaze' within a decidedly problematic framework."

68. Brandum notes that *Ishtar*'s style is relatively restrained compared to her previous films, which had "displayed an eye for striking framing and juxtaposition of shots between edits that have the tendency to appear ostentatious. In *Ishtar*, her use of film grammar calls attention to itself due to its sheer minimalism" (148).

69. Other critics, too, have picked up on these parallels; Rachel Abramowitz, for one, has described *Mikey and Nicky* as a "kind of endless Nichols-and-May routine" (79).

70. See Bordwell for a full discussion of staging's deprecation in film theory: "To this day critics praise a virtuoso piece of editing while remaining oblivious to far more subtle and powerful passages of staging" (8). Sarah Kozloff and, more recently, Jennifer O'Meara discuss the antidialogue tendencies that frame talk as "literary" or more broadly uncinematic. As O'Meara puts it, "Cinema is still considered a visual rather than a verbal medium" (1).

71. See, for instance, production designer Paul Sylbert's complaints that May "was not prepared to use" the locations to their advantage, among other highly critical comments shared with Beatty biographer Peter Biskind (*Star* 349).

72. Steve Martin, speaking of this line, notes that Nichols and May were the first to ironize the new obsession with "relationships": "The word came into being in the early sixties. Now we can't get rid of the word, but it was the first time I ever heard [the word] satirized" (qtd. in Nachman 323).

73. The film's release met with condemnation from the American-Arab Anti-Discrimination Committee and calls for a boycott of the film on the basis of its use of "ethnic and religious slurs" (Hull).

74. "So when I first met him, and he wanted me to do *Heaven Can Wait*, and this is how he presented it: He said, '[I]t's a remake, and uh, I'm not going to be in it, and uh, I'm putting this together as a starring vehicle for Muhammad Ali, and it's about a boxer who he dies and he goes to heaven but it's a mistake so they bring him back but his body's been cremated so they put him in the body of a CEO whose wife has just murdered him and then the CEO comes back and when the CEO comes back, everyone in the *movie* sees the CEO is the CEO but the audience sees the CEO as Mohammad Ali and then Mohammad Ali meets a girl and then a boxer dies and he goes in his body. . . . [I]t's a love story. . . . Everybody turned it down'" (May, "Elaine May on Warren Beatty").

75. See Nicholas Godfrey for an account of the (outsized) ways critical commentary shaped both the reception of individual films and broader production trends in New Hollywood. As he notes, the influence exerted by "the critical and discursive environment surrounding theatrical exhibition" remains an understudied area of analysis (2).

76. BoxOffice Mojo reports that *Ishtar* made $14 million against a $55 million budget. Other sources put the budget at closer to $51 million. May has since disputed these budget figures.

77. The tweets have since been deleted but exist as screenshots.

78. According to production manager Nigel Wooll, Beatty "wouldn't stop the camera. Instead of going to Take 1, Take 2, Take 3, he'd do it all in one run until the roll of film ran out, after 10 minutes. He would just say, 'Do it again,' 'Do it again,' 'Do it again.'" But this created its own peculiar problems. Wooll recalls, "We burned out three camera motors because they overheated. I've never, ever burned out a camera motor before or since. It was extraordinary" (Biskind, "Thunder").

79. See Smukler's *Liberating Hollywood* for a detailed account of the double standards studios imposed upon women filmmakers in the 1970s.

80. See Rebecca Sheehan and Courtney Brannon Donoghue for sociohistorical accounts of the ways industry "lore" and logics have militated against women filmmakers and burdened them with outsized demands.

81. See Karina Longworth's podcast series on Platt's career and Aaron Hunter's book *Polly Platt*.

82. As reported by *Deadline* in November 2019: "Dakota Johnson . . . told me she plans to do a movie for Elaine May, a recent Tony winner who is getting behind the camera again at age 86 to direct Johnson in a movie called *Crackpot*" (Hammond). Asked in early 2024 about the status of the project, Johnson confirmed that it is still in development (Newman).

An Interview with Elaine May |

Elaine May in conversation with HFA director Haden Guest following a screening of *Mikey and Nicky*, November 12, 2010, transcript, https://harvardfilmarchive.org/calendar/mikey-and-nicky-2010–11. Bracketed insertions in the transcript that indicate applause, laughter, and so on have been removed, and the names or initials of speakers have been added.

HADEN GUEST: Good evening, ladies and gentlemen. If you could please take your seats. Thank you all for coming tonight. I'd like to welcome you to a very, very special evening that we've been eagerly awaiting and hoping for, and we're so glad to be here to celebrate an artist whose extraordinary talents and inspiring career have made her a legend—many, many times over. I'm speaking, of course, of Ms. Elaine May, who is with us tonight.

As you know, Ms. May made a name for herself, first of all, through her incredible and pioneering work with Mike Nichols, with whom she formed what was, without a doubt, one of the most popular and deeply influential comedy teams of the 20th century. During their unforgettable five years together, May and Nichols redefined the course of American comedy through their urbane, irreverent and breathtakingly intelligent blend of satire that gleefully poked fun at the absurdities of everyday life in 50s America. May and Nichols's hilarious skits had a shaping influence on contemporary stand-up comedy, it should be noted and is often stated. And also offered a wonderful showcase for Ms. May's innate talents as a commanding actress, able to transform herself in a flash and with total conviction from coy teenager to intractable telephone operator, to a ruthlessly nagging mother. And on Sunday we're going to be seeing one of Ms. May's really great performances in *A New Leaf*, her first film, which you absolutely cannot miss.

Equally showcased, however, in her work with Nichols, was Ms. May's absolute brilliance as a writer. Her talent and ability to craft keenly insightful, even we could say intellectual, but at the same time totally hilarious comedy. Since the end of her fabulous collaboration with Nichols, Ms. May has flourished both as a highly successful and prolific playwright of such major works as *Not Enough Rope*, *Adaptation* and *Adult Entertainment*, and a much sought after screenwriter. But equally important, and the reason why we're here tonight, Ms. May also directed four boldly original and wonderfully eccentric films: *A New Leaf*, *The Heartbreak Kid*, *Ishtar* and tonight's film, *Mikey and Nicky*, that together have won her a prominent place in the history of the post-studio era American cinema as one of the unsung, and still I would say, underappreciated heroines of the so-called New Hollywood of the 70s.

Ms. May was, of course, one of the few women directors active in Hollywood during the 70s, but she was also one of the few directors making significant work in comedy, an important tradition in American cinema. It was of course comedy that was the home to some of Hollywood's greatest directors: Wilder, Lubitsch, and Sturges, many, many others. But it was, by the 70s, a genre that had long been abandoned as a source for major work. And it was here that Elaine May entered, and she did by embracing a notably offbeat and often quite dark, we can say, mode of comedy that brought to a new level the fearlessness that had defined her work with Nichols, which was characterized by a bold, and even affectionate, embrace of often taboo subject matter. As a result, many I would say, of Ms. May's films were often met with stunned disbelief and misinterpretation. And it's only in recent years, only with events such as this, that Ms. May's films have been rediscovered as the major works which indeed they are. And tonight's film from 1976, *Mikey and Nicky*, offers a really splendid expression of the true fearlessness and brilliant iconoclasm that defines Ms. May's films. It's her first original screenplay. And it offers a dark and intense portrait of friendship and masculinity that's quite complex and fascinating, and, I'd say, among Ms. May's most intense and rewarding works. It was dismissed perfunctorily by the mainstream press. It was mishandled criminally by the studio, Paramount, and it's a film that deserves to be far better known. Thankfully, it's often cited as being recognized gradually, to the point that today, it's often cited as one of the great films of the 1970s. It has dark comic touches, but it is in no way a comedy, as you'll see. It's a tough and unflinching film. We're really proud that we can see it tonight in a gorgeous new print that comes to us, thanks to Julian Schlossberg, who I would ask us to applaud in person but, unfortunately, he can't be here tonight. But I really want to thank him. And this print is now becoming part of the Harvard Film Archive collection, available for future generations of students and scholars and, of course, film lovers such as all of you. Tonight is extra special because we also have two additional guests, who I just want to thank for being with us tonight and acknowledge. I speak, of course, of Mr. Stanley Donen who is here.

Just about a year ago, we had a wonderful retrospective, celebrating the amazing work of Stanley Donen. And so it's always an honor to have him with us. But we also have a wonderful actress whose Oscar-nominated performance in *The Heartbreak Kid* we're going to see on Sunday: Ms. Jeannie Berlin.

But now, with no further ado, I give you Ms. Elaine May.

ELAINE MAY: Thank you. Thank you. Can you hear me? Cuz that's important. It was because of this film, *Mikey and Nicky*, that Stanley Donen asked me out.

I haven't seen this movie in twenty years. So I hope I enjoy it.

The milieu, the people in this movie, are actually my milieu. I'm a Chicago, sort of gangster girl. And the events aren't exactly true, but they have happened. So it's sort of a kind of a true story, but nobody knows this about me except you guys, and I'm afraid you all have to die.

I'm so pleased that you've come. I've never introduced a film before, so I don't know exactly what to say except that I hope you like it, and I'll see you after the show.

Postscreening Discussion

HG: Thank you so much for sharing this film with us and for being here tonight. And I wanted to ask you, just to begin, what you think of seeing this film for the first time in so long? How did it strike you tonight?

EM: I keep remembering that during this film, Paramount Pictures changed hands. A new head came in. And he thought this was a comedy. And I don't know why they made it. I really don't. The guy who made it was a guy named Frankie Yablans and he was also a gangster, and probably knew my family. But when they saw it, it was a bad moment.

HG: You mentioned Frank Yablans, and I've heard it said that he was originally—he was then President of Paramount. He was originally cast in the Ned Beatty role as the hitman, correct?

EM: Yes, we cast the head of Paramount, Frank Yablans, in Ned Beatty's part, and he was fantastic. He would drive up. We were rehearsing, I forget where, he would drive up in his limo and get out and then join the cast and rehearse. And the real owner of Paramount, a man named Charles Bluhdorn, called him and said, "What are you doing? You're the head of Paramount, you're playing a killer in a movie? And it's a small part?"

So he quit. And we got Ned, who was actually really good, really close to what those guys are like. Because they're just little businessmen.

HG: No, he's absolutely fantastic. And, I mean, the film is such a radical film, I think, in so many ways. But also I think, perhaps most interestingly, in the way that it breaks from your previous films. It's the intensity of it, the sort of nervous style, and the presence and role of Cassavetes is of course major in this film. And I was wondering if you could talk about how you came to Cassavetes. And also, of course, Peter Falk. Because these were two actors who were very much identified with a certain style of performance. So how did you come to Cassavetes? And how did you work with him? Is it true that much of the performances were improvised?

EM: No, you can't. It's not possible to improvise this because—although it seems not to be—it's really plot-driven.

HG: Absolutely.

EM: So you can only fit these small incidents to tell the relationship, and they have to be narrow, and they have to really say exactly what they're going to say. You can't ad-lib around them. But I met John Cassavetes way before this, because he tried to give me $10,000. Because Screen Gems had foolishly put him in charge of giving money to artists, and he just gave money away. He said, "I'm going to give you $10,000" and I said, "I don't want it." I didn't know him at the time. He knocked on my door and he said, "I'm giving you $10,000. You don't have to do anything." And I became immediately paranoid and I said, "I don't want it." And he wrote me a letter.

HG: Sounds like the beginning of the film.

EM: Well, we became friends because he felt that I was more insane than he was. And we just were friendly. And when this movie—which I had written, which actually is sort of based on an incident with these guys. He and Peter read the film, because Peter was a friend too, and he was great. And then he said he wanted to do some movie of his own first, because I forget why. And I was so pissed that I was going to cast somebody else. And I read people for a year, and then in the end he said, "I'm done with my film, I really apologize." And then I just cast him, because nobody else could play him. He was so perfect for that part, for that Italian guy. He's a terrific actor.

HG: What role did he have in shaping the sort of nuances of this character, of Nicky?

EM: He just got him. I mean, he was just born to play him. He and Peter were very good friends, so that was very helpful. Everything went wrong on this, because they kept cancelling the movie. Because they kept looking at the dailies and seeing that it wasn't a comedy. And they would cancel it, and then we would be off. And somewhere I read that I was able to shoot as much as I wanted, but I just really kept shooting because they would cancel it, we would go off, we would start. And he was really great about it. He stuck it out. And the only thing he demanded was that he'd be good. So things would break down, it would be late, they wouldn't show up, etcetera, he would stand by. But if he thought he wasn't good in a take, he would just be furious at me. So that was his demand, which is an absolutely reasonable demand. He just was very good in the part. He got it immediately, he immediately understood who the guy was. Didn't try to make him nice, didn't try to make him mean[.] Just understood that it was about the friendship with Peter, and he would tease Peter anyway so . . .

HG: Now I want to talk about these characters. Because, throughout your films, so many of your characters are adults who seemed trapped in a sort of extended childhood. I think of the character you play so wonderfully in *A New Leaf*, the botanist, or Walter Matthau, sort of Little Lord Fauntleroy in the same film. I also think of Charles Grodin in *The Heartbreak Kid*. And of course Beatty and Hoffman in *Ishtar*. But it's in this film, I think, that we find the purest expression of this idea. Especially Cassavetes, who's being given glasses of milk, who's got his lollipops in his comic books, and all of these sort of motifs. I'm wondering what attracts you to this type of character, this sort of man-child if you will?

EM: Well, these are these guys.

I mean, these are really what these guys are like. The Jews in the— The syndicate was very big—[i]f you really want to know this. This is just hearsay, but the syndicate was very big in Chicago. And we were sort of part of it. And we were very good friends with my uncle who had an ulcer. Was very good friends with the Italian guy who once blew up a cleaning store because they were rude to my aunt Fanny.

But they were in the back of the store. They weren't killed, thank God. And they just, they're like this. They fascinated me because the wives sort of know and don't know. You think they *have* to know, and they kind of do know, but they don't. You can't finger a guy unless you're a friend. You can't get close to him. So only friends can finger you. And yet, they allow friends in, yet they get fingered. Yet they're very interesting men because their friendships are very tight. Their bonds are really with other guys. And they've known each other for years. They don't totally trust each other if they don't know each other a long time. That's who will betray you, your best friend. It's the only one who can.

HG: This idea of betrayal is also a constant. Betrayal is a constant in your films. Friends betraying friends. Here, though, you add another layer of complexity in the way that other people are brought in too. The way the wife is made an accessory to the murder at the end. I think it's quite extraordinary.

EM: Well, she would have been[.] I don't know if they're interesting as people. I don't know if they're interesting as characters, but they were interesting to me as people. Because I can't tell you why they behave that way. But I really can tell you, hardly ever said this firmly about something I've done, that that's truly what they're like. What you see, if you're at all interested in these guys—and they're small-time—the killers are really trying to get enough money to get a bank going, open a bookie joint. They're just small-time businessmen, but they have to have a stake, and it's a terrible job. They're out all night, there's no place to park. If they hire another guy, then they gotta split with the other guy. So it's fascinating because it's just like business. It's not as bloody as Wall Street, but it's bloody.

HG: Now the character of the Don, or *Don* I think is too strong a word. One of the mob bosses is played by one of the great—considered together with Lee Strasberg to be one of these great acting coaches—Sandy Meisner.

EM: Sandy Meisner, yeah.

HG: I was wondering if you could talk about the decision to cast him. Like Lee Strasberg, this is only one of two films that he's in.

EM: I wanted Kazan.

And Kazan said, "I'll do it if I can play the killer."

HG: Everybody wants to be the killer.

EM: I thought he was wrong for the killer. Bill Hickey, who was the guy sitting down, is also an acting teacher. But Sandy Meisner did it because acting teachers like to act. Everybody likes to act, really. And it was a good part. It was a longer part originally. The sound in this is very odd, because occasionally I can't hear any of it. Because the mix is strange. But when he came back to loop, the reason I had to cut him down: his voicebox had been taken out. He had his surgery. It was really awful. So I had to cut his scene down. But I wanted him because he was perfect. Acting teachers are perfect for this. They're on top of it. They know you. I knew he knew how to do it. It's good to get good actors. It gives you a lot less trouble.

HG: It's an interesting motif. Think of Lee Strasberg, and here as well—the acting coach as criminal. Speaking of criminal acts, I guess I'd like to know a bit more about—This is a film like so many of your films, it's sort of wrapped in myth and legend. I've heard so many times, told again and again, how, you know, the acting was improvised, you corrected that. But something else that's constantly repeated is the story of why Paramount so terribly mishandled this film. The film was given only two days release, perfunctory, and part of that is there's some sort of myth that somehow two reels of the negative were absconded with.

EM: Yes, someone stole them. But when Paramount changed hands, the feeling between the two people—Yablans and Barry Diller—was very bitter, to put it mildly. And of course, Barry Diller thought this was a comedy. Thinking this was a comedy really killed me. I mean, it was a cheap little movie and I don't know why they let me do it. I think because *A New Leaf* was so successful, and I promised to do another one, or *Heartbreak Kid*—whatever I did this after. But they were also horrified to see it. Because they laughed, and then they realized that it wasn't funny. I mean, that it was funny but that it wasn't gonna turn out well. So they had a fight with each other. I think Diller said to you [sic] Yablans: "Why have you let her make this movie?" And Yablans said to Diller, as was his want [sic]: "Fuck you." And then they had a big fight. I mean they really, really were at each other's throats. So when Yablans left, they sued me. I have no idea why. I really don't know why. But the only thing I can think of—I know this sounds insane—is that Diller was from television. And I was cutting the negative. And the only thing I could think of was that he didn't understand that you had to cut the negative to make a movie. And I never knew why. And I once asked him, because we became, of course, friends: "Why did you sue me?" He said, "I don't know." He said, "I was so miserable."

HG: So the story of the stolen negative, then, was a fabrication?

EM: No, the negative was stolen.

HG: Can you tell us a little bit of—?

EM: Well, the feeling was, because there was a strange call that they were going to come and seize the movie. And then someone stole the negative. And then, when they came to seize the movie they came—There's an old law in New York that you can bring a sheriff with you[.] I don't mean to laugh, but a sheriff with a gun came in to this editor who said the negative and a reel was stolen. They went into a mix studio with the sheriff and a gun, and the mix studio was furious and wouldn't turn over the reels. They were very stupid about it. But they cost me a fortune. I think they were pissed at each other. I think Yablans treated Diller very badly. And this wasn't a comedy. That was the biggest thing that this wasn't, was it [sic] was a comedy. I think, I don't know. I keep looking for reasons, but I never did understand it exactly. And it went on for a very long time because they couldn't recut it, because they didn't have the negative. But I want to tell you that no matter how you recut this, it wasn't going to be a comedy anyway.

HG: Now you did, though, you were able to put the film back in the form that we saw tonight?

EM: Yes.

HG: So how did that happen?

EM: Well, the law firm for Paramount decided—We're in a meeting and the lawyers came in and said, "We have turned this into a criminal case, because we have said that the negative may have crossed state lines."

And Barry Diller said, "Are you crazy? You want us to be the only studio that jails a director for going over budget? Are you crazy?" And they actually dropped the suit for that. They were so terrified. My lawyer also. They were so terrified that I would be jailed, that they went back and they tried to take it back. And the judge said, "If you're using this court, in a civil matter, if you're using it, we will come down very hard on you." So they just let the subpoena ride. And they said, "Okay, just have the negative show up" although I didn't know where it was. But I put the word out and it came back and we put it together.

It was a very odd movie. Its history almost overcame it. And it was odd to them because it was about guys. It was a gangster movie. It was funny only for a limited amount of time. And I wanted it to look streety, grainy. It was shot at night, you know, sort of like it was captured. And they didn't like that. They just didn't expect it. They didn't like it. They didn't. They weren't prepared for it.

HG: This is a film, to me, that is truly ahead of its time. Looking at the reviews that came out, in the way in which it was completely misunderstood. So to see it with an audience today, and to feel the appreciation is really rewarding. I'd like to take some questions from the audience. Open it up. And if you just raise your hand. There are audience mics. There's one there in the back?

EM: Ask me anything.

AUDIENCE 1: Thank you. I guess I'm a little dense, or was a bit dense tonight watching this, because and maybe it's partly because I had in my head the program notes which said two guys fleeing a contract killer. And I couldn't get out of my head until really late in the movie that, you know, the extent of the betrayal. The phone call early at the bar, I sort of didn't get it. And then I didn't get the phone call to his wife's house. I guess what I'm sort of wondering: are viewers meant not to quite get it as it's going along or, in fact, was I just too dense?

EM: Sort of, yes. Because it's one theme all the way through, and you want to have something to keep somebody wondering. Because once you know, then that emotional bond between the two of them is broken for sure. So yes, it was sort of deliberate.

AUDIENCE 1: Thanks.

HG: We have a question here in the front. I'm sorry, it's behind you, then we'll get to you. No, no, go ahead. Go ahead.

AUDIENCE 2: First of all, I wanted to say I am such a fan. I could gush so much about all your work and I saw *Adult Entertainment*. When I saw you wrote it, I dragged my dad [to it] in New York. I know so many things you've done, so many people quote [your films], even *The Birdcage*, Madonna and Twyla, and I mean, people still do that all the time. I just wondered what you thought of the state of comedy today, and if there were writers you particularly admired. Given that you are clever and smart and just what you think.

EM: Well, I don't think any funny movies were really funny until about 1980. I watch old movies and I cannot understand what's funny about them. There are funnier comedies now, sporadically, than there were. But comedies were always like this. There are, you know, like ten movies that are supposed to be funny and then one that is. *There's Something About Mary* was funny. God, it had the best sight gag in it I've ever seen. But then there are just movies that pick up on that, and they're not. So comedy is observational now. And also, the comedic joke now is that men are sort of boyish bears and hang around and drink beer and all like that together, and that joke wears out but it's funny. *Knocked Up* was a very funny movie. So I think the state of comedy is just as good and bad as it's ever been. It's never been great.

HG: In the front then. Here's the microphone, please.

AUDIENCE 2: Well it was when you were doing your stand-up with Nichols. You have to admit, it was great.

EM: Oh, thank you. Actually stand-up was pretty good. It was the movies. There were some really really great stand-up guys. Carlin and Bruce and Mort Sahl. Actually in the clubs there were a lot of funny people. But somehow that didn't translate to movies, because movies were supposed to be for dumber people, you know?

AUDIENCE 2: Do you think that's the reason? Or do you think it has something to do with the structure of the cumbersome Hollywood film mechanism? Because stand-ups—

EM: That's a good question.

AUDIENCE 2: Yeah.

EM: But you can tell the same story very wittily, or you can tell it very stupidly. Most comedies really have to do with what can go wrong. So, if you have a drama, some man comes in and takes a girl and rips her bra off and opens her blouse. If you have a comedy, some man rips the blouse off and then can't quite get the bra open, and then has to turn it around in front and then . . .

So, really, the kind of comedy that would be like stand-up is just detail. The real truth, the real observation, of how difficult it is to get anything done.

AUDIENCE 2: I'd like to know what you're working on now.

EM: A play. I have a play that I'm hoping is going to—Three one-acts. One with Woody Allen, and mine, and God I don't even remember who the third one is. Who is it?

AUDIENCE: Ethan Coen!

EM: Ethan Coen? Yes, Ethan Coen. I've never met him. But a very funny play. And we're going to do that, as soon as we have a director. So I just finished that. And then I do a lot of ghostwriting, which I can't talk about.

HG: We have some questions in the middle of the house.

AUDIENCE 3: Yes, I wondered when this movie first came out: I wonder if you remember some of the reviewers['] comments, misguided as they were, that sort of stick in your mind. They're probably a good transcript of the period. And I wondered if you remembered some of them that you could share with us.

EM: Say the last part again.

AUDIENCE 3: I was curious about the reviewers, the reviews of this movie when it first came out? If there were comments that, as misguided as they might have been, stick in your mind as good transcripts.

EM: What sticks in my mind, of course, is that I try not to read reviews. But what sticks in my mind is that they didn't like it and they were bewildered. But every once in a while, some critic would call it the best in ten years, one of the best, every once in a while. But it would have to be a critic. Reviewers reviewed the lawsuit, literally. It was in *New York* magazine. Actually, that was at the moment where reviewers had gone past the movie to the fact of who you were married to, and that you had been drinking, you know, all through the summer. So it was the lawsuit, really, and the lawsuit got magnificent reviews.

HG: You could pass the mic to the gentleman behind you. Had a question there.

AUDIENCE 4: I was a little baffled by what it seemed to me [was] a kind of strange conflict in the presentation of the characters. Because on the one hand, they seem, comically, like a bit of ordinary males, etcetera. On the other hand, there is a scene of—really a kind of psychopathic scene. They're kind of ordinary guys talking with the usual male stuff, but at the same time, and I think that, probably, that's the way I took it, was intentional on your part. Because it does have an element of psychopathic madness.

EM: Well they're not ordinary guys at all. You know, it's interesting, as I watched the movie—and I didn't think of this when I was making it—but I started thinking of the teasing that now goes on in high schools, where students just kill themselves because of the cruelty. The casual cruelty of high school of a certain age. These aren't ordinary guys, because ordinary guys grew up to be sort of grown-ups. And also, the milieu that they come out of, really, is a whole other background. Whatever you're born into seems like the normal world. I mean, to me, it was years before I realized that people didn't have a gun in the house and, you know, they didn't arrest you for booking every week. That seemed to me the way the world was. So to these guys, I mean, at some point somebody can overcome their world, but if you can't, that's the world. The world is that you're going to die. That you can get killed. That family is everything, but it's the family that's going to kill you. It's a very contradictory world. It really is. My mother once said of the mafia, she said, "There's no such thing as the mafia" because we were the syndicate. She said, "There's no such thing as the mafia," and then she said finally, she said: "Those Italians were our drivers." And I thought, look at the amount of ambition each one had, the competition between the two of them. And my mother was an absolutely respectable woman. She really was. She would never, she didn't curse, her eyebrows will go up, but that was her world, that was the world she had been born into. It's sort of like cannibals. You think: "How can they eat each other?" But that's what they do.

HG: We have a question in the back there.

AUDIENCE 5: What makes it so difficult for the audience to recognize themselves in a work of art? To be more aware that it's about us and not about someone else?

EM: You answer that. You try, go ahead.

HG: Gosh, I mean, I think it's sometimes, I personally feel like sometimes it's very hard to look in the mirror. And so that's the same sort of discomfort I think that we find, you know, seeing a film that has a real honesty. I think the idea, for instance, of the way in which long-term friendships can turn into betrayal, I think is incredibly true.

EM: But also, you know, we're kind of primitive and then we learn sort of not to be. But everybody has felt that you take a little kid to the street and he won't go. And you plead with him and you say, "Come on, let's go." But in your heart, you know you can just pick him up and carry him across the street if you want to. You can let a woman slap you in the face if you're a guy because you can beat the shit out of her. So, we learn, we're civilized. These instincts are, we learn more than this. Civilization teaches us something, and really rouses, and probably, we're genetically sort of tuned to that, or else we would just sort of kill each other. But these guys, they don't have that overlay. Nobody teaches them that other way. They have a code. No kidding, it really is a code. God knows what it is because it's constantly broken. But they live by it, but they break it. In that way, we're like that. It's sort of like you say, "You've got to call me!" "I will call you, absolutely," and you never do.

And you mean it when you say it. And these guys sort of, they have a perverted sense of what honor is. But they do have a sense of what honor is. But they have to survive. It's really sort of like *The Godfather* at a tiny level. You kind of have to survive. And they also have a leader. They might kill him, but while he's in charge, he's the leader. They have to kill him. They can't ever demote him. They can never go to the law. They have to police each other. So, I recognize that in me, but I'm fortunately too weak to carry it out.

HG: We have a question right there.

AUDIENCE 6: Is it okay if I ask you a question outside the film? Sort of a broader question. I just wanted to know how you knew that this was what you wanted to do? All of this. I don't just mean making the movie, I mean.

EM: You mean why I wanted to do this film?

AUDIENCE 6: No. Outside of that. Even from the beginning of your career, if you will, when did you sort of know, "Okay, this is what I'm going to do in my life"?

EM: You mean this film or my career?

AUDIENCE 6: Your career.

HG: Comedy as a vocation. How did you come upon—?

EM: I just belonged to Second City. And that's what we did. We would take suggestions from the audience. And you really can't do a serious scene from a suggestion. So it evolved, and I think you discover that you're funny. And then you think there's a living in this. And you go on. I don't know that anybody decides to be a comedian. Maybe they do. Anybody here? Nobody wants to be a stand-up? You're kidding. Really? Oh well.

AUDIENCE: It's Harvard!

EM: There.

HG: Amy's got a question.

AUDIENCE 7: Hi, I just wanted to know if you could say what neighborhood that is in Chicago. And also, whether the guys in your family saw this film and what they thought of it?

EM: My ears closed on the train which was stalled for an hour. Say it to me a little louder.

AUDIENCE 7: I wanted to know what neighborhood it was in Chicago. I was struck by the Black dance club, and I was wondering if it was the South Side? And then I was also just wondering if the guys in your family saw the film and what they thought of it.

HG: So first, the location of the film. Was it in Chicago?

EM: Was it where?

HG: Was it in Chicago, the film? I thought it was in Philadelphia.

EM: No, we couldn't shoot it in Chicago. We had to shoot it in Philadelphia. You know, these guys, particularly Chicago mob guys, are sort of gone now. But really, these gangs mean nothing now. It's just drugs now. I've lost touch with everybody. We left Chicago. When you leave Chicago, you kind of leave that world, because that really was what Chicago was like. It was really—

AUDIENCE 7: You mean the South Side or? I was just wondering about the specific part of Chicago.

HG: What was the specific part of Chicago you were from?

EM: We were from the near North Side, but it didn't matter where you were from. My mother once said that no crime that was continued— that is, prostitution or vice—could be continued without the cooperation of the police. Gas station robberies, one-timers. I don't know if she was right or not, but she was right in Chicago.

HG: There's a question right there on the edge.

AUDIENCE 8: Given that you've been in comedy, but that the content of this later film of yours seems the most directly about your early years, had you been wanting to make a drama or another movie about criminals earlier on? And what was your thinking as you went from comedies to this?

EM: I'm really glad you asked me that question. I wrote this as a one-act play for Second City because at that time we would run out and somebody would put out a one-act. And I thought, "What can I do with two guys and no scenery?" And I wrote it and it was a one-act and I thought, "Gee, this would be a good movie." Because with all the scenes where there was no scenery, I could actually put scenery in, and I could put in cemeteries, etcetera. So that was how I wrote it. I had no ambition to write about gangsters. They were just people in the company who could do that. It was good kibbitz that way, as we said.

HG: Let's take this one up here and then we'll get to you in the middle.

AUDIENCE 9: It seems like the experience making this film for you might have been traumatic and exhausting, as far as your experience with the studio and their sort of misunderstanding and interference. I wonder how you felt? I wonder if that is, in fact, how you felt once the film was finished and released? And at that point, when the film was done, how you thought about making your next film, and working with the studio again? Were you encouraged at all, or just felt victimized or exhausted? So how did you sort of proceed after this film, to write and direct your next?

EM: I had a friend you probably heard of named Shel Silverstein, who once said to me, "If there was an earthquake, and all the film was destroyed, and all the editors were destroyed, will you be happy? Or would you be distraught?" And I said, "I'd be so happy."

Yes, it was awful. Not that the movie was hard, but all of it was very difficult. And John Cassavetes once said to me, "If you want to avoid the lawsuit." He was so smart this way—you wouldn't think it. "Give a party, and invite all the important people you know, including the head of the studio." And I said, "Oh, are you crazy? I'm not giving a party! Such an idiot. That's ridiculous. I'm not inviting these people to my house and blah blah blah." But he was right. Had I given a party and invited everybody, they couldn't have sued me. It's such a tiny community. But I didn't.

HG: Well we're giving a party right now. Right in the middle, the gentleman in the striped shirt.

AUDIENCE 10: Speaking of partying and Cassavetes, part of the Cassavetes mythology is that there was a lot of carousing in the 70s with Peter Falk and Ben Gazzara. And I'm just wondering what the work atmosphere was like in your recollections? Was it that everybody just did their twelve-hour days and it looked like a lot of night shoots? Did everybody just go home and go to bed or was there carousing?

EM: He was so great that I fired my cameraman four times because he was terrible. And John actually shot—There's a handheld shot of a car pulling up. Such a steady handheld shot that you could jumpcut it. It was so incredible. We couldn't get a good decent cameraman and he said, "Don't make me shoot my own death. Please."

He was wonderful. He never groused. He would be pissed at me if he wasn't good in a take. But then he didn't grouse. He would just go huffily to his trailer. But I don't know any actor, any star, any actor who would, to make the movie work, be so un-grousy, if I may use that term. I don't know who he—Where did you hear this, incidentally?

AUDIENCE 10: *Carousing.*

HG: Oh, *carousing.*

EM: Oh carousing? No. Peter Falk caroused. John Cassavetes never did, no. John didn't carouse. He looked like he would carouse.

And all the girls on the movie had a crush on him and were sort of hurt because he didn't carouse. But he wasn't a carouser, and he was a big joker. I mean, he really was funny. He liked to imitate Groucho Marx, which wasn't a romantic thing for most women.

But he was not a carouser.

HG: Go ahead.

AUDIENCE 11: The series is celebrating your direction. But you're such a wonderful comic actress. And I think the last movie that I can recall seeing you in was *Small Time Crooks*, the Woody Allen movie. Do you have any plans or hopes to act in a movie again?

EM: Well, I don't know that you plan that. I mean, I could plan to, but it wouldn't mean nothing.

AUDIENCE 11: Would you like to?

EM: You have to like the part. Because people do ask you to do parts, but they're really, you know, nothing that you can do anything with. They sort of just take your time. So yes, I would like to do something if I felt that my doing it would contribute to the movie, she said.

You know, it's like: I would be naked if it was part of the plot.

HG: Let's take two more questions and we'll—Right there. Yes, please. With the beard, yes.

AUDIENCE 12: You wanted to make the narrative seem captured and give that impression. That's what I've always thought. And I think that's one of the great strengths of the film.

EM: You're speaking very shyly. And I'll tell you, my ears have actually closed since I got off the train.

HG: The mic's on. Just speak into the mic.

AUDIENCE 12: Sorry. When you said that you wanted the narrative to seem captured, I thought that's one of the great strengths of the film, that it seems very casual, the performances. They just turn on you on a dime. And that's one of the most striking things about it, except for the scene right after Cassavetes sleeps with his girlfriend and she turns the lights back on. And it's a very bright scene, very stark, and the way it's lit seems different from a lot of the other scenes. And so it strikes me as kind of a very stylized moment in a narrative that otherwise seems, a film that otherwise seems almost like it's grabbed or documentary or whatever. Did you approach the scene that way when you scripted it, the visuals of it?

EM: You mean the scene where he screws the girl?

AUDIENCE 12: Yeah and it's all dark.

EM: I mean you're not going to have him screw a girl—you sort of have to stylize it.

AUDIENCE 12: I meant when the lights come on, after.

HG: In the white room with the flowers.

EM: Well, yes, it was so dark, the movie, that you really—I hope I'm answering your question because . . .

HG: He means the actual staging of the scene. The actual staging of the apartment itself seems more deliberate, one could say, than the rest of the film.

EM: Well, it was. It was, because to deal with these three people in that situation, it had to be deliberately staged. It was not true. I mean I don't know if somebody would go in the kitchen in that situation, but it had to be done. It was probably not truthful staging as the other was, but it was staged.

HG: Right. I'm struck by the film—does seem, at some levels—has this incredible improvisational sort of sense, this sense of spontaneity. But seeing it again, I'm struck at how carefully structured it is. The way the first and last scenes echo each other with the doors. Peter Falk trying to break in the first one, and Cassavetes at the end. It's so carefully and precisely constructed, in fact.

EM: I think its improvisational sense comes from the fact that A: They were friends and B: They were perfect for the part.

HG: Right.

EM: He's Greek, he's Jewish. And also, I had noticed that when men fight, they never punch, they push. And that *was*. I just let them go till they knew they weren't going to punch. So that actually, as John threw the coat and kept provoking, the lines weren't, but that action was. Because they knew they had to fight and we knew that there wasn't— Because they say you want a fight coordinator—And I've never seen a fight—and I've seen them—where a guy punched a guy. I've never seen it. They push, they wrestle. I don't know where it came—Westerns, I think.

HG: Blame it on John Wayne perhaps.

EM: That movement was improvised.

HG: Okay, well look. Please join me in thanking Elaine May. Please come back tomorrow, for *Ishtar*. Thank you.

Feature Films

A New Leaf (1971, United States)
Paramount Pictures
Director: Elaine May
Screenplay: Elaine May
Producers: Hillard Elkins, Howard W. Koch, Joseph Manduke
Photography: Jay Gayne Rescher
Editor: Don Guidice, Fredric Steinkamp
Music: Neil Hefti
Cast: Walter Matthau (Henry Graham), Elaine May (Henrietta Lowell), Jack Weston (Andy McPherson), James Coco (Uncle Harry), George Rose (Harold), Dorris Roberts (Mrs. Traggert)
Screen
102 mins.

The Heartbreak Kid (1972, United States)
Palomar Pictures
Director: Elaine May
Screenplay: Neil Simon
Producer: Edgar J. Scherick
Photography: Owen Reizman
Editor: John Carter
Music: Garry Sherman
Cast: Charles Grodin (Lenny Cantrow), Jeannie Berlin (Lila Cantrow), Cybill Shepherd (Kelly Corcoran), Eddie Albert (Mr. Corcoran), Audra Lindley (Mrs. Corcoran)
106 mins.

Mikey and Nicky (1976, United States)
Paramount Pictures
Director: Elaine May

Screenplay: Elaine May
Producer: Michael Hausman
Photography: Victor J Kemper, Bernie Abramson, Lucien Ballard
Editors: John Carter, Sheldon Kahn
Music: John Straus
Cast: Peter Falk (Mikey), John Cassavetes (Nicky), Ned Beatty (Kinney), Carol
Grace (Nellie), Rose Arrick (Annie), Joyce Van Patten (Jan), Stanford Meisner
(Dave Resnick), William Hickey (Sid Fine)
106 mins.

Ishtar (1987, United States)
Columbia Pictures
Director: Elaine May
Screenplay: Elaine May
Producer: Warren Beatty
Photography: Vittorio Storaro
Editors: Richard P. Cirincione, William H. Reynolds, Stephen A. Rotter
Music: Paul Williams, Dave Grusin, Bahjawa
Cast: Dustin Hoffman (Chuck Clarke), Warren Beatty (Lyle Rogers), Charles
Grodin (Jim Harrison), Isabelle Adjani (Shirra Assel), Jack Weston (Marty
Freed), Carol Kane (Carol), Tess Harper (Willa Rogers)
107 mins.

Documentary

Mike Nichols: American Masters (2016, United States)
Witnesses Documentary Productions, Bennington Productions, Thirteen Pro-
ductions
Distributor: American Masters
Director: Elaine May
Producer: Julian Schlossberg, Michael Kantor, Roy Furman
Photography: Michael Claeys
Editors: Michael Claeys, Phillip Schopper
54 mins.

Abramowitz, Rachel. *Is That a Gun in Your Pocket? The Truth about Female Power in Hollywood.* New York: Random House, 2000.

Allison, Sue, and Claudia Dowling. "Dustin on Warren: Hoffman Talks about Singing, Stardom, Sex, and All That Garbage. Beatty Listens." *Life*, May 1987, 63–68.

Amburn, Ellis. *The Sexiest Man Alive: A Biography of Warren Beatty.* New York: Harper, 2002.

Anderson, Melissa. "Elaine May." *4 Columns*, Jan. 18, 2019. https://4columns.org/anderson-melissa/elaine-may.

Bakhtin, Mikhail. *Speech Genres.* Austin: University of Texas Press, 1979.

Bart, Peter. *Infamous Players: A Tale of Movies, the Mob (and Sex).* New York: Weinstein Books, 2011.

Bart, Peter. "The Rise and Fall of David the Didactic." *Variety*, June 23, 1997. https://variety.com/1997/voices/columns/the-rise-and-demise-of-david-the-didactic-1117859590/.

Barthes, Roland. *S/Z.* New York: Hill and Wang, 1974.

Beeston, Alix. "Kathleen Collins . . . Posthumously." In *Incomplete: The Feminist Possibilities of the Unfinished Film*, edited by Alix Beeston and Stefan Solomon, 245–69. Oakland: University of California Press, 2023.

Bennett, Bruce. "Hope and Crosby, They Were Not." *Wall Street Journal*, May 16, 2011. https://www.wsj.com/articles/SB100014240527487035091045763256330228224472.

Berlant, Lauren. *Cruel Optimism.* Durham, NC: Duke University Press, 2011.

Berliner, Todd. *Hollywood Incoherent: Narration in Seventies Cinema.* Austin: University of Texas Press, 2010.

Biskind, Peter. *Easy Riders, Raging Bulls: How the Sex-Drugs-and-Rock 'n' Roll Generation Saved Hollywood.* New York: Simon & Schuster, 1998.

Biskind, Peter. "Madness in Morocco: The Road to *Ishtar*." *Vanity Fair*, Jan. 7, 2010. https://www.vanityfair.com/news/2010/02/ishtar-excerpt-201002.

Biskind, Peter. *Star: How Warren Beatty Seduced America.* New York: Simon & Schuster, 2011.

Biskind, Peter. "Thunder on the Left: The Making of *Reds.*" *Vanity Fair*, Mar. 2006. https://archive.vanityfair.com/article/2006/3/thunder-on-the-left-the -making-of-reds.

Blum, David. "The Road to *Ishtar.*" *New York*, Mar. 16, 1987, 34–43.

Bondanella, Peter. *A History of Italian Cinema*. London: Bloomsbury, 2009.

Bordwell, David. *Figures Traced in Light: On Cinematic Staging*. Berkeley: University of California Press, 2005.

BoxOffice Mojo. "*Ishtar.*" BoxOfficeMojo.com; accessed Mar. 21, 2024. https:// www.boxofficemojo.com/release/rl1264223745/weekend/.

Brady, John. *The Craft of the Screenwriter: Interviews with Six Celebrated Screenwriters*. New York: Simon & Schuster, 1981.

Brandum, Dean. "Cartographies of Catastrophe: Elaine May's *Ishtar.*" In Heller-Nicholas and Brandum, *ReFocus*, 139–62.

Brody, Richard. "Elaine May Talks about *Ishtar.*" *New Yorker*, Apr. 1, 2016. https://www.newyorker.com/culture/richard-brody/elaine-may-talks-about -ishtar.

Brody, Richard [@tinyfrontrow]. "Happy Birthday to Elaine May, Studio Victim." *Twitter*, Apr. 21, 2019, 2:18 p.m., https://twitter.com/tnyfrontrow/ status/1120029126088437760?lang=bg.

Brody, Richard. "A Lovingly Obsessive Tribute to Mike Nichols, by Elaine May." *New Yorker*, Jan. 29, 2016. https://www.newyorker.com/culture/ richard-brody/a-lovingly-obsessive-tribute-to-mike-nichols-by-elaine-may.

Brody, Richard. "To Wish upon *Ishtar.*" *New Yorker,* Aug. 9, 2010. https://www .newyorker.com/culture/richard-brody/to-wish-upon-ishtar.

Brooks, Vincent. "A Wave of Their Own: Jewish Filmmakers Invented the New Hollywood." *Jewish Film & New Media: An International Journal* 7.1 (Spring 2019): 48–80.

Bryer, Jackson R., and Ben Siegel, eds. *Conversations with Neil Simon*. Jackson: University Press of Mississippi, 2019.

Butler, Isaac. *The Method: How the Twentieth Century Learned to Act*. New York: Bloomsbury, 2022.

Canby, Vincent. "Love Turns 'New Leaf' at Music Hall." *New York Times*, Mar. 12, 1971. https://www.nytimes.com/1971/03/12/archives/love-turns-new-leaf-at-music-hall.html.

Canford, Tom. *A Fever of the Mad: A Movie Publicist Works with Francis Coppola, Elaine May, John Cassavetes, Peter Falk, and Richard Gere and Survives to Tell the Tale!* Edited by Jonathan May. Hollow Square Press, 2003.

Carlin, Matt. "Throw a Problem at a Situation: The Films of Elaine May." *MUBI*, Jan. 22, 2019. https://mubi.com/notebook/posts/throw-a-problem-at-a -situation-the-films-of-elaine-may.

Carr, Jeremy. "*Mikey and Nicky*: Elaine May and the Cassavetes Connection." In Heller-Nicholas and Brandum, *ReFocus*, 119–38.

Cavell, Stanley. *Pursuits of Happiness: The Hollywood Comedy of Remarriage.* Cambridge, MA: Harvard University Press, 1984.

Chew-Bose, Durga. "In Hollywood." Thisrecording.com, Aug. 31, 2012. http://thisrecording.com/today/2012/8/31/in-which-joan-didion-and-john-gregory-dunne-write-together.html.

Chihaya, Sarah. *The Ferrante Letters: An Experiment in Collective Criticism.* New York: Columbia University Press, 2020.

Chung, Evan. "Ishtar Didn't Die a Natural Death." *Slate,* June 7, 2019. https://slate.com/culture/2019/06/ishtar-movie-failure-elaine-may-sabotage.html.

Cohen, Mitchell S. "The Heartbreak Kid." *Film Quarterly* 26.4 (Summer 1973): 60–61.

Coleman, Janet. *The Compass: The Improvisational Theatre That Revolutionized American Comedy.* Chicago: University of Chicago Press, 1990.

Colvin, Brandon. "The Other Side of Frontality: Dorsality in European Art Cinema." *New Review of Film and Television Studies* 15.2 (2017): 191–210.

Cooper, Peter. *"Aren't You Gonna Die Someday?": Elaine May's "Mikey and Nicky," an Examination, Reflection, and Making Of.* BearManor Media, 2019.

Courogan, Carrie. "Decades Later, the World Is Catching Up to Elaine May." *Glamour,* Nov. 4, 2019. https://www.glamour.com/story/elaine-may-profile.

Dargis, Manohla. "The Marvelous Ms. Elaine May." *New York Times,* Jan. 21, 2019. https://www.nytimes.com/2019/01/21/movies/elaine-may-movies.html.

Darrach, Brad. "On the Road to *Ishtar.*" *People,* May 25, 1987, 102–7.

Deighan, Samm. "Kneeling on Glass: Elaine May's *A New Leaf* (1971) as Screwball Black Comedy." In Heller-Nicholas and Brandum, *ReFocus,* 85–103.

Donoghue, Courtney Brannon. "Gendered Expectations for Female-Driven Films: Risk and Rescue Narratives around Warner Bros.' *Wonder Woman.*" *Feminist Media Studies,* July 2019, 1–17.

Dyer, Richard. "Resistance through Charisma: Rita Hayworth and *Gilda.*" In *Women in Film Noir,* edited by Ann Kaplan, 91–99. London: BFI, 1980.

Ebert, Roger. "Reds." RogerEbert.com, Jan. 1, 1981. https://www.rogerebert.com/reviews/reds-1981.

Elsaesser, Thomas. "The Pathos of Failure: American Films in the 1970s; Notes on the Unmotivated Hero." In *The Last Great American Picture Show: New Hollywood Cinema in the 1970s,* edited by Thomas Elsaesser, Alexander Horwath, and Noel King, 279–92. Amsterdam: Amsterdam University Press, 2004.

Ephron, Nora. *I Remember Nothing: And Other Reflections.* New York: Knopf, 2010.

Falk, Peter. *Just One More Thing: Stories from My Life.* New York: Carroll and Graf, 2006.

Falk, Peter. "Interview (1976)." *Mikey and Nicky.* Criterion, 2019. DVD.

Fine, Marshall. *Accidental Genius: How John Cassavetes Invented the American Independent Film.* New York: Hyperion, 2005.

Finstad, Suzanne. *A Private Man: Warren Beatty*. New York: Three Rivers Press, 2005.

Fitzpatrick, Veronica. "Blind Date: *A New Leaf* (1971)." *Bright Wall/Dark Room* 75 (2019). https://www.brightwalldarkroom.com/2019/09/06/elaine-may-new -leaf-1971/.

Ford, Jessica. "Feminist Cinematic Television: Authorship, Aesthetics, and Gender in Pamela Adlon's *Better Things*." *Fusion* 14 (2018): 16–29.

Gaines, Jane. *Pink-Slipped: What Happened to Women in the Silent Film Industries?* Urbana: University of Illinois Press, 2018.

Gainey, Christian. "Bill Murray Had to Invent His Entire Tootsie Roll." *Slashfilm*, Apr. 20, 2022. https://www.slashfilm.com/733266/shows-like-stranger-things -you-definitely-need-to-stream/.

Genette, Gérard. *Narrative Discourse: An Essay in Method*. Ithaca, NY: Cornell University Press, 1993.

Getti, Claudio. "Elena Ferrante: An Answer?" *New York Review of Books*, Oct. 2, 2016. https://www.nybooks.com/online/2016/10/02/elena-ferrante-an-answer/.

Gilbey, Ryan. "From Improv to *Ishtar*: The Many Lives of Comedy Genius Elaine May." *The Guardian*, Nov. 18, 2018. https://www.theguardian.com/stage/2018/ nov/18/elaine-may-comic-writer-director-the-waverly-gallery-broadway.

Godfrey, Nicholas. *The Limits of Auteurism: Case Studies in the Critically Constructed New Hollywood*. New Brunswick, NJ: Rutgers University Press, 2018.

Goldstein, Patrick. "They All Have a Secret." *Los Angeles Times*, Mar. 15, 1998. https://www.latimes.com/archives/la-xpm-1998-mar-15-ca-28947-story.html.

Grace, Carol. *Among the Porcupines*. New York: Random House, 1992.

Grant, Catherine. "Secret Agents: Feminist Theories of Women's Film Authorship." *Feminist Theory* 2.1 (2001): 113–30.

Gregory, Molly. *Women Who Run the Show: How a Brilliant and Creative New Generation of Women Stormed Hollywood*. New York: St. Martin's, 2002.

Grindon, Leger. *The Hollywood Romantic Comedy*. New York: Wiley-Blackwell, 2011.

Grodin, Charles. *It Would Be So Nice If You Weren't Here: My Journey through Show Business*. New York: William Morrow, 1989.

Gruen, John. "More Than Elaine May's Daughter." *New York Times*, Jan. 7, 1973. https://www.nytimes.com/1973/01/07/archives/more-than-elaine-mays -daughter-more-than-elaine-mays-daughter.html.

Guest, Haden. "The Comic Vision of Elaine May." Harvard Film Archive, November 12–14, 2010. https://harvardfilmarchive.org/programs/the-comic -vision-of-elaine-may.

Guest, Haden. A postscreening discussion about *Ishtar*. Harvard Film Archive, Nov. 13, 2010.

Guest, Haden. A postscreening discussion about *Mikey and Nicky*. Harvard Film Archive, Nov. 12, 2010.

Haber, Joyce. "Elaine May Has a Thing on Not Talking to Press: Nonlinear Interview with Elaine May." *Los Angeles Times*, July 7, 1968. In *Nichols and May: Interviews*, edited by Robert E. Kapsis, 45–48. Jackson: University Press of Mississippi, 2020.

Hammond, Pete. "Notes on the Season." *Deadline*, Nov. 1, 2019. https://deadline.com/2019/11/dark-waters-oscar-jokers-tarantino-scprsese-ray-romano-1202774166/.

Harris, Mark. *Mike Nichols: A Life*. New York: Penguin, 2021.

Haskell, Molly. "Are Women Directors Different?" In *Women and the Cinema: A Critical Anthology*, edited by Karyn Kay and Gerald Peary, 429–35. New York: Dutton, 1977.

Haskell, Molly. Foreword to *Screwball: Hollywood's Madcap Romantic Comedies*, by Ed Sikov, 10–13. New York: Crown, 1989.

Haskell, Molly. *From Reverence to Rape: The Treatment of Women in the Movies*. 3rd ed. Chicago: University of Chicago Press, 2016.

Haskell, Molly. "A Long Day's Journey into Buddy-Buddy Land." *Village Voice*, Jan. 3, 1977, 36–37.

Haskell, Molly. "The Mad Housewives of the Neo–Woman's Film: The Age of Ambivalence, Revisited." In *When the Movies Mattered: The New Hollywood Revisited*, edited by Jonathan Kirshner and Jon Lewis, 18–35. Ithaca, NY: Cornell University Press, 2019.

Hastie, Amelie. "Genealogies of a Decade: Classifying and Historicizing Women of the New Hollywood." In *Women & New Hollywood: Gender, Creative Labor, & 1970s American Cinema*, edited by Aaron Hunter and Martha Shearer, 185–206. New Brunswick, NJ: Rutgers University Press, 2023.

Heilpern, John. "Out to Lunch with Stanley Donen." *Vanity Fair*, Feb. 22, 2013. https://www.vanityfair.com/hollywood/2013/03/stanley-donan-singin-in-the-rain.

Heller-Nicholas, Alexandra. "In/Significant Gestures: Elaine May, Screen Performance, and Embodied Collaboration." In Heller-Nicholas and Brandum, *ReFocus*, 165–80.

Heller-Nicholas, Alexandra. Introduction to Heller-Nicholas and Brandum, *ReFocus*, 1–20.

Heller-Nicholas, Alexandra, and Dean Brandum, eds. *ReFocus: The Films of Elaine May*. Edinburgh: Edinburgh University Press, 2019.

Hennefeld, Maggie. *Specters of Slapstick and Silent Film Comediennes*. New York: Columbia University Press, 2018.

Hoberman, J. "Flaunting It: The Rise and Fall of Hollywood's 'Nice' Jewish (Bad) Boys (Part 4)." *FilmLinc Daily*, Oct. 31, 2011. https://www.filmlinc.org/daily/flaunting-it-the-rise-and-fall-of-hollywoods-nice-jewish-bad-boys-part-4/.

Hoberman, J. "Hollywood's 'Jew Wave.'" *Film at Lincoln Center*, Nov. 3–13, 2011. https://www.filmlinc.org/series/hollywoods-jew-wave/.

Hoberman, J. "In *Mikey and Nicky*, Elaine May Nails a Pair of Desperate Characters." *New York Times*, July 2, 2019. https://www.nytimes.com/2019/07/02/movies/elaine-may-mikey-and-nicky.html.

Hoberman, J. "May Days." *Village Voice*, Feb. 14, 2006. https://www.villagevoice.com/2006/02/14/may-days/.

Honeycutt, Kirk. "Women Filmmakers: Will They, Too, Be Allowed to Bomb?" *New York Times*, Aug. 6, 1978. https://www.nytimes.com/1978/08/06/archives/women-film-directors-will-they-too-be-allowed-to-bomb-women.html.

Hull, Victor. "'Ethnic and Religious Slurs': Arab Community Criticizes *Ishtar.*" *Los Angeles Times*, May 16, 1987. https://www.latimes.com/archives/la-xpm-1987-05-16-ca-9491-story.html.

Hunter, Aaron. *Polly Platt: Hollywood Production Design and Creative Authorship*. Berlin: Springer, 2022.

Hunter, Aaron, and Martha Shearer, eds. *Women & New Hollywood: Gender, Creative Labor, & 1970s American Cinema*. New Brunswick, NJ: Rutgers University Press, 2023.

Johnson, Kevin. "Elaine May: 'Do You Mind Interviewing Me in My Kitchen?'" *New York Times*, Jan. 8, 1967. https://www.nytimes.com/1967/01/08/archives/movies-elaine-may-do-you-mind-interviewing-me-in-the-kitchen.html.

Kael, Pauline. "New Thresholds, New Anatomies." *New Yorker*, Dec. 16, 1972, 126, 128, 130, 131.

Kael, Pauline. "Noodles." *New Yorker*, Jan. 6, 1987, 101–5.

Kael, Pauline. "Pleasing and Punishing." *New Yorker*, Jan. 8, 1972, 74–78.

Kapsis, Robert E., ed. *Nichols and May: Interviews*. Jackson: University Press of Mississippi, 2020.

Kashner, Sam. "Who's Afraid of Nichols & May?" *Vanity Fair*, Jan. 13, 2013. https://archive.vanityfair.com/article/2013/1/whos-afraid-of-nichols-may.

Kercher, Stephen E. *Revel with a Cause: Liberal Satire in Postwar America*. Chicago: University of Chicago Press, 2006.

King, Geoff. *Film Comedy*. New York: Columbia University Press, 2002.

Kirshner, Jonathan. *Hollywood's Last Golden Age: Politics, Society, and the Seventies Film in America*. Ithaca, NY: Cornell University Press, 2012.

Kirshner, Jonathan, and Jon Lewis, eds. *When the Movies Mattered: The New Hollywood Revisited*. Ithaca, NY: Cornell University Press, 2019.

Kolker, Robert. *A Cinema of Loneliness: Penn, Kubrick, Scorsese, Spielberg, Altman*. New York: Oxford University Press, 1988.

Kozloff, Sarah. *Overhearing Film Dialogue*. Berkeley: University of California Press, 2000.

Krefting, Rebecca. *All Joking Aside: American Humor and Its Discontents*. Baltimore, MD: Johns Hopkins University Press, 2014.

Kundera, Milan. *Testaments Betrayed: An Essay in Nine Parts*. New York: Perennial, 2001.

Lane, Christina. "Susan Seidelman's Contemporary Films: The Feminist Art of Self-Reinvention in a Changing Technological Landscape." In *Indie Reframed: Women's Filmmaking and Contemporary American Independent Cinema*, edited by Linda Badley, Claire Perkins, and Michele Schreiber, 70–86. Edinburgh: Edinburgh University Press, 2016.

Lauzen, Martha M. "The Celluloid Ceiling: Employment of Behind-the-Scenes Women on Top-Grossing U.S. Films in 2022." Center for the Study of Women in Television and Film, San Diego State University, 2023.

Lennard, Dominic, R. Barton Palmer, and Murray Pomerance, eds. *The Other Hollywood Renaissance*. Edinburgh: Edinburgh University Press, 2020.

Lloyd, Robert. "As a TV Series, Woody Allen's 'Crisis in Six Scenes' Offers Many Pleasures of a Woody Allen Movie." *Hartford Courant*, Sept. 29, 2016. https://www.courant.com/la-et-st-crisis-in-six-scenes-review-20160927-snap-story.html.

Lonergan, Kenneth. "Playwright Kenneth Lonergan on the Genius of His *Waverly Gallery* Star Elaine May." *Variety*, May 23, 2019. https://variety.com/2019/voices/columns/kenneth-lonergan-waverly-gallery-elaine-may-1203223871/.

Longworth, Karina. "Polly Platt: The Invisible Woman." You Must Remember This, May 25–July 27, 2020, http://www.youmustrememberthispodcast.com/episodes/2020/7/pollyplattarchive28.

"The Making of *Mikey and Nicky*." *YouTube*, Aug. 28, 2020. https://www.youtube.com/watch?v=qIXnPfJfy_I.

Malone, Noreen. "When Joan Didion Was a Hollywood Schlockmonger." *Slate*, Dec. 23, 2021. https://slate.com/culture/2021/12/joan-didion-dead-hollywood-movies-career.html.

Margulies, Ivone. Comment on "Elaine May: Dispassionate," by Joe McElhaney. Unpublished draft, Oct. 3, 2019.

Martin, Adrian. *Mise-en-Scène and Film Style: From Classical Hollywood to New Media Art*. London: Palgrave, 2013.

Martin, Angela. "Refocusing Authorship in Women's Filmmaking." In *Women Filmmakers: Refocusing*, edited by Jacquelin Levitin, Judith Plessis, and Valerie Raoul, 29–37. New York: Routledge, 2003.

May, Elaine. *Adaptation*. New York: Dramatists Play Service, 1971.

May, Elaine. *Adult Entertainment*. New York: Samuel French, 2002.

May, Elaine. *Death Defying Acts*. New York: Samuel French, 1992.

May, Elaine. "Elaine May in Conversation with Mike Nichols." *Film Comment*, July–Aug. 2006. https://www.filmcomment.com/article/elaine-may-in-conversation-with-mike-nichols/.

May, Elaine. "Elaine May Interviews Kenneth Lonergan." *Vulture*, June 3, 2019. https://www.vulture.com/2019/06/elaine-may-interviews-kenneth-lonergan.html.

May, Elaine. "Elaine May on Warren Beatty & *Heaven Can Wait.*" *American Film Institute*, Jan. 6, 2010. https://www.youtube.com/watch?v=TV1uA2iVpTg.

May, Elaine. "Elaine May Salutes Mike Nichols at the AFI Life Achievement Award." *American Film Institute*, Oct. 8, 2010. https://www.youtube.com/watch?v=AgjBxiDmJyU.

May, Elaine. *In and Out of the Light.* In *Power Plays: Three One-Act Plays.* New York: Samuel French, 1998.

May, Elaine. *Ishtar.* 1985. Screenplay. Internet Archive. https://web.archive.org/web/20071010132952/http://www2.uclaextension.edu/writers/pdfs/scriptlib/ishtar.pdf.

May, Elaine. *Mikey and Nicky.* 1976. Screenplay. Script Slug. https://www.scriptslug.com/script/mikey-and-nicky-1976.

May, Elaine. *A New Leaf.* 1971. Screenplay. Script Slug. https://www.scriptslug.com/script/a-new-leaf-1971.

May, Elaine. *Not Enough Rope.* New York: Samuel French, 1992.

May, Elaine. *Power Plays: Three One-Act Plays.* New York: Samuel French, 1998.

May, Elaine. *Taller Than a Dwarf.* New York: Samuel French, 1999.

May, Elaine. *The Way of All Fish.* In *Power Plays: Three One-Act Plays.* New York: Samuel French, 1998.

May, Elaine. "Who's Who in the Cast." Program for Kenneth Lonergan's play *The Waverly Gallery*, Golden Theatre, New York, 2018–19.

May, Elaine. "*In the Spirit* Promo." Video, 5:28. YouTube. Posted by Westchester Films, July 25, 2013. https://www.youtube.com/watch?v=r5GGOaWFZx4.

McDonald, Tamar Jeffers. *Romantic Comedy: Boy Meets Girl Meets Genre.* New York: Columbia University Press, 2007.

McElhaney, Joe. "Elaine May: Dispassionate." *Screening the Past* 45 (December 2020). https://www.screeningthepast.com/issue-45-first-release/elaine-may-dispassionate/.

Meyers, Julian. "Four Dialogues 4: On Elaine May." *Open Space*, Aug. 28, 2009. https://openspace.sfmoma.org/2009/08/four-dialogues-4-on-elaine-may/.

Mike Nichols. American Masters, season 30, episode 1. Aired Jan. 29, 2016. https://www.pbs.org/wnet/americanmasters/mike-nichols-about-the-film/6065/.

Mittell, Jason. *Complex TV: The Poetics of Contemporary Television Storytelling.* New York: New York University Press, 2015.

Moore, Elise. "Elaine May's Male Gaze." *Bright Wall/Dark Room* 75: *Elaine May* (2019). https://www.brightwalldarkroom.com/2019/09/13/elaine-may-male-gaze/.

Morrison, James. "Elaine May's Awkward Age." In *Women & New Hollywood: Gender, Creative Labor, & 1970s American Cinema*, edited by Aaron Hunter and Martha Shearer, 113–26. New Brunswick, NJ: Rutgers University Press, 2023.

Mulvey, Laura. "Visual Pleasure and Narrative Cinema." *Screen* 16.3 (Oct. 1975): 6–18.

Nachman, Gerald. *Seriously Funny: The Rebel Comedians of the 1950s and 1960s.* New York: Pantheon, 2003.

Naremore, James. *Acting in the Cinema.* Berkeley: University of California Press, 1988.

Neale, Steve, and Frank Krutnik. *Popular Film and Television Comedy.* New York: Routledge, 1990.

Newman, Nick. "Dakota Johnson Confirms Elaine May's Crackpot Is Still in Development." *The Film Stage,* Feb. 8, 2024. https://thefilmstage.com/dakota -johnson-confirms-elaine-mays-crackpot-is-still-in-development/.

Ngai, Sianne. *Theory of the Gimmick: Aesthetic Judgement and Capitalist Form.* Cambridge, MA: Harvard University Press, 2020.

Nichols, Mike, and Elaine May. *An Evening with Mike Nichols and Elaine May.* Mercury Records, 1960.

Nichols, Mike, and Elaine May. *Improvisations to Music.* Mercury Records, 1958.

Nichols, Mike, and Elaine May. "Nichols and May at the 1959 Emmys." 11th Primetime Emmy Awards. NBC, Hollywood, May 6, 1959. YouTube. https:// www.youtube.com/watch?v=0Bk6VcZpboc.

Nichols, Mike, and Elaine May. *Nichols and May Examine Doctors.* Mercury Records, 1961.

North, Michael. *Machine-Age Comedy.* Oxford: Oxford University Press, 2008.

O'Farrell, Tim. "Spectral Elaine May: The Later Mike Nichols Collaborations and the Myth of the Recluse." In Heller-Nicholas and Brandum, *ReFocus,* 202–17.

O'Meara, Jennifer. *Engaging Dialogue: Cinematic Verbalism in American Independent Cinema.* Edinburgh: Edinburgh University Press, 2018.

Oswalt, Patton. "Patton Oswalt on *Mikey and Nicky.*" *Mikey and Nicky.* Criterion, 2019. DVD.

Paszkiewicz, Katyryzna. *Genre, Authorship, and Contemporary Women Filmmakers.* Edinburgh: Edinburgh University Press, 2019.

Perman, Chad. "But We Can Sing Our Hearts Out: *Ishtar* (1987)." *Bright Wall/ Dark Room* 75: *Elaine May* (2019). https://www.brightwalldarkroom.com/ 2019/09/23/elaine-may-ishtar-1987/.

Pickett, Rex [@rexpickett]. "It's not a gender thing . . . " Twitter, Sept. 1, 2020, 12:41 p.m. https://twitter.com/carriecourogen/status/1300840632852926464/ photo/1.

Pickett, Rex [@rexpickett]. "Last add on *Ishtar* . . . " Twitter, Aug. 30, 2020, 9:17 p.m. https://twitter.com/RexPickett/status/1300241257898283009.

Press, Joy. "Promising Young Women." *Vanity Fair,* Mar. 1, 2021. https://www .vanityfair.com/hollywood/2021/02/promising-young-women-1970s-women -directors.

Probst, Leonard. "Elaine May: Funny Is Closer to Life." In *Off Camera: Leveling about Themselves,* 129–35. New York: Stein and Day, 1975.

Quart, Barbara. *Women Directors: The Emergence of a New Cinema*. New York: Praeger, 1988.

Raban, Nathan. *My Year of Cinematic Flops: The AV Club Presents One Man's Journey Deep into the Heart of Cinematic Failure*. New York: Scribner, 2010.

Rabinowitz, Peter. "Betraying the Sender: The Rhetoric and Ethics of Fragile Texts." *Narrative* 2.3 (1994): 201–13.

Rice, Robert. "A Tilted Insight." *New Yorker*, Apr. 15, 1961, 47–75.

Rich, B. Ruby. "In the Name of Feminist Film Criticism." In *Multiple Voices in Feminist Film Criticism*, edited by Diane Carson, Linda Dittmar, and Janice R. Welsch, 27–47. Minneapolis: University of Minnesota Press, 1994.

Rickey, Carrie. "Why Elaine May Is a National Treasure." *The Forward*, Sept. 23, 2018. https://forward.com/culture/film-tv/410742/why-elaine-may-is-a-national-treasure/.

Ritchie, Jack. "A Green Heart." *Alfred Hitchcock's Mystery Magazine* 8.3 (Mar. 1963): 34–51.

Rivlin, Michael. Interview by Leonard Probst. *Millimeter* 3.10 (Oct. 1975): 16–18, 46. Reprinted in "Elaine May: Too Tough for Hollywood? Or, the Benadryl Tapes." In *Nichols and May: Interviews*, edited by Robert E. Kapsis, 80–85. Jackson: University Press of Mississippi, 2020.

Rosenbaum, Jonathan. "The Mysterious Elaine May: Hiding in Plain Sight." Jonathanrosenbaum.net, Mar. 10, 2022. https://jonathanrosenbaum.net/2022/03/21700/.

Rottenberg, Dan. "Elaine May . . . or She May Not." *Chicago Tribune*, Oct. 21, 1973, 55–58.

Schlossberg, Julian. "Commentary." *Mikey and Nicky*. Criterion, 2019. DVD.

Schlossberg, Julian. *Try Not to Hold It against Me: A Producer's Life*. Foreword by Elaine May. New York: Beaufort Books, 2023.

Scott, A. O. "What Would Ernst Lubitsch Have Done?" *New York Times*, June 15, 2003. https://www.nytimes.com/2003/06/15/movies/film-what-would-ernst-lubitsch-have-done.html.

Searles, Jourdain [@judysquirrels]. "she's a genius. She's one of our most underrated filmmakers. she's a living legend. she's basically made only classics. one of the greatest to ever do it." Twitter, Oct. 1, 2023, 9:48 p.m., https://twitter.com/judysquirrels/status/1708660215304823107.

Sheehan, Rebecca. "'One Woman's Failure Affects Every Woman's Chances': Stereotyping Impossible Women Directors in 1970s Hollywood." *Women's History Review*, 2020, 1–23.

Shelley, Peter. *Neil Simon on Screen: Adaptations and Original Scripts for Film and Television*. Jefferson, NC: McFarland, 2015.

Shepherd, Cybill. *Cybill Disobedience*. New York: Harper Collins, 2000.

Shepherd, Richard F. "Elaine May: Q&A about Her Play." *New York Times*, Sept. 23, 1962. In *Nichols and May: Interviews*, edited by Robert E. Kapsis, 17–20. Jackson: University Press of Mississippi, 2020.

Shone, Tom. *Blockbuster: How Hollywood Learned to Stop Worrying and Love the Summer*. New York: Free Press, 1994.

Simon, Carly. *The Charlie Rose Show*. May 22, 2000. https://charlierose.com/videos/29051.

Simon, Neil. Screenplay of *The Heartbreak Kid*. Aug. 1972. Neil Simon Papers, Library of Congress, Washington, DC.

Smukler, Maya Montañez. "Hollywood Can't Wait: Elaine May and the Delusions of 1970s American Cinema." In Heller-Nicholas and Brandum, *ReFocus*, 41–62.

Smukler, Maya Montañez. *Liberating Hollywood: Women Directors and the Feminist Reform of the 1970s American Cinema*. New Brunswick, NJ: Rutgers University Press, 2018.

Sparrow, Norbert. "'I Let the Audience Feel and Think': An Interview with Rainer Werner Fassbinder." *Cineaste* 2 (1977): 20–21.

Stevens, Brad. "*Ishtar*, Elaine May, and the Road Not Taken." *BFI*, Apr. 24, 2017. https://www2.bfi.org.uk/news-opinion/sight-sound-magazine/comment/bradlands/ishtar-elaine-may-road-not-taken.

Stevens, Brad. "Male Narrative / Female Narration: Elaine May's *Mikey and Nicky*." *Cineaction!* 31 (1993): 74–83.

Stevens, Chuck. "Chronicle of a Disappearance." *Film Comment*, Mar.–Apr. 2006, 46–53.

Stevens, Kyle. "Elaine May: Subverting Machismo Step by Tiny Step." In *The Other Hollywood Renaissance*, edited by Dominic Lennard, R. Barton Palmer, and Murray Pomerance, 189–203. Edinburgh: Edinburgh University Press, 2020.

Stevens, Kyle. *Mike Nichols: Sex, Language, and the Reinvention of Psychological Realism*. Oxford: Oxford University Press, 2015.

Stevens, Kyle. "The Politics of Humor, from Dry to Wet." *Cultural Critique* 112 (Summer 2021): 1–23.

Stevens, Kyle. "Tossing Truths: Improvisation and the Performative Utterances of Nichols and May." *Critical Quarterly* 52.3 (2010): 23–46.

Thomas, Marlo. *Growing Up Laughing: My Story and the Story of Funny*. New York: Hyperion, 2010.

Thompson, Thomas. "Whatever Happened to Elaine May?" *Life*, July 28, 1967. In *Nichols and May: Interviews*, edited by Robert E. Kapsis, 35–44. Jackson: University Press of Mississippi, 2020.

Tobias, Andrew. "Elaine May: A New Film, but Not a New Leaf." *New York*, Dec. 6, 1976. In *Nichols and May: Interviews*, edited by Robert E. Kapsis, 86–96. Jackson: University Press of Mississippi, 2020.

Warren, Ethan. "Still Heartbroken after All These Years: *The Heartbreak Kid* as Elaine May's Master Class." *Bright Wall/Dark Room* 75: *Elaine May* (2019). https://www.brightwalldarkroom.com/2019/09/09/the-heartbreak-kid-elaine-may1972/.

Wasson, Sam. *Improv Nation: How We Made a Great American Art*. New York: Harper, 2017.

White, Patricia. *Women's Cinema, World Cinema: Projecting Contemporary Feminisms*. Durham, NC: Duke University Press, 2015.

Wilson, Edmund. *The Sixties: The Last Journal, 1960–1972*. New York: Noonday, 1994.

Wood, Robin. *Hollywood from Vietnam to Reagan*. New York: Columbia University Press, 2003.

Woods, Travis. "A Tunnel in My Head: *Mikey and Nicky* (1976)." *Bright Wall/Dark Room 75: Elaine May* (2019). https://www.brightwalldarkroom.com/2019/09/17/elaine-may-mikey-and-nicky-1976/.

Wyatt, Justin. *High Concept: Movies and Marketing in Hollywood*. Austin: University of Texas Press, 1995.

Zeitlin, David. "A Homely Non-Hero, Dustin Hoffman, Gets an Unlikely Role in Mike Nichols' *The Graduate*." *Life*, Nov. 24, 1967.

Zolandz, Lindsay. "Heaven Can Wait: The Hidden Genius of Elaine May." *The Ringer*, May 14, 2019. https://www.theringer.com/pop-culture/2019/3/14/18245240/elaine-may-life-career-mike-ishtar-nichols-mikey-and-nicky-heartbreak-kid-a-new-leaf.

camerawork: an unforgiving light, 76, 76; in *The Heartbreak Kid*, 53–58, 70; in *Ishtar*, 96, 110; in *Mikey and Nicky*, 68–70, 78–79; in *A New Leaf*, 1, 43, 44, 50, 109–10; optimized for laughs, not visual spectacle, 98; of Warren Beatty in *Reds*, 110–11, 128n78

capitalism and market-driven culture, 102–3

Cassavetes, John, 24, 67–68, 70, 86, 133, 144–46; Falk and, 67–68, 82, 87, 88, 133, 134, 144, 146; Haden Guest on, 132–34; May on, 70, 88, 133, 144–46; May's interactions with, 9, 24, 25, 70, 82–84, 87, 88, 132–33, 144; in *Mikey and Nicky*, 24, 25, 67–68, 70, 82–85, 87, 88, 132, 144–46

casting, 111; *Ishtar*, 87–90; against type, 90, 104, 111

characters in May's films: May's relations with, 5; similarities between May and, 21. *See also* female characters in May's films

characters played by May, 38. See also *Enter Laughing*: May in

Chicago, 142–43; May and, 84, 131; May in, 17, 143

cinematography. *See* camerawork

cliché, 42; absence of, 74; avoiding, 26, 58; evacuation of, 75; functions of, 73; *Mikey and Nicky* and, 73–75; reversal of, 53

Cohen, Alexander H., 20–21

Coleman, Janet, 18–20, 25, 27, 28, 80

Collins, Kathleen, 118

comedy: dark, 3, 36, 131 (see also *New Leaf*); May on, 26; romantic, 42, 52, 67 (*see also* buddy films); unromantic, 41–43. *See also specific topics*

comedy albums, 22

comedy of discomfort, 63. See also under *Heartbreak Kid*

comedy of remarriage, 7, 42

comic incrementalism, May's, 26; "step by tiny step," 26–28, 33, 93

comic method of May, 26–27. *See also* comic incrementalism

comic stonewalling, 39

"Comic Vision of Elaine May, The" (Guest), 6. *See also* Guest, Haden

communists, 103, 111

Compass Players, 17–19, 25, 80

Cooper, Peter, 84–85

coupledom, 66, 67, 69. *See also specific topics*

Crackpot, 37, 119

Crisis in Six Scenes, 37, 38, 40

crowding out the couple, 49

cynicism, 67

Dale, Esther (May's pseudonym), 35

"Dangerous Business" (song), 92, 106, 107

dark comedy, 3, 36, 131. See also *New Leaf*

detail, May's attention to, 33, 84

director, May as, 3, 6, 9, 11, 40, 43–44; characterizations of, 4, 6, 9, 11, 70, 84; comedy and, 130; compared with other directors, 6, 9, 11, 13; conversion to director, 6; criticism of, 84; "director jail" and, 4, 8; films she directed, 2, 5, 21, 130 (*see also specific films*); "first-time director and a woman," 43; handling of time, 39; improv and, 24 (*see also* improvisation); infamous aspects of her direction, 69; May's thoughts and feelings about directing, 115–16; method(s)/approach(es), 2, 3, 24, 26–28; misdirection, 3; obstacles facing, 9, 12, 14, 103; radical dimensions of her filmmaking, 6–7; and shifting nature of her comic targets, 5

directors, 11; feminism, gender, and, 13, 109 (*see also* female directors)

Directors Guild of America, 16, 122n1

discomfort and comedy, 5, 34, 62, 63, 79, 80. See also *Heartbreak Kid*

dispassionate approach, 6, 57, 79, 121

distance from characters, keeping, 53, 56, 57, 59, 79, 95. See also under *Heartbreak Kid*

Donen, Stanley, 17

Donoghue, Courtney Brannon, 114, 118

double standards, 12, 13, 18, 115

"dumb men," 104; May's fetish for, 14

Eastwood, Clint, 13
Elsaesser, Thomas, 91–92
Enter Laughing: Carl Reiner and, 21;
May in, 21, 38, *38*
ethnic interloper, Lenny Cantrow, 61, *61*
ethnic jokes, 33, 100–101
ethnic stereotypes, 101–2
*Evening with Mike Nichols and Elaine
May, An* (comedy album), 22
exclusion, Hollywood's logics of, 113–16

failures of films, 112, 113, 116; the bathos
of failure, 91–96. *See also* box-office
flops/bombs; *Ishtar*: failure of; success
Falk, Peter: Cassavetes and, 67–68, 82,
87, 88, 133, 134, 144, 146; Haden
Guest on, 132, 146; May on, 88, 133,
145; May's interactions with, 25, 82, 85,
87, 133; in *Mikey and Nicky*, 24–25,
67–68, 80–82, 85, 87, 88, 132, 133, 146
fatalism in May's plays, 34–35
female characters: abjection and abjectness of, 14, 43, 79–80, *80*; in May's
films, 20. *See also specific characters*
female directors, 8, 108, 116, 117,
122n1; auteurism and, 12; challenges
faced by, 113–17; conflicts with
Paramount, 9; expectations placed on,
13–15; gender, sexism, and, 109, 110,
113–16, 122n3; "It's not *your* turn,"
116–18; May and other, 4, 13–16, 109;
May compared with other, 9, 11; pattern of "failure" by contemporary, 109;
paucity of, 4, 130
femininity, 40, 81
feminism, May and, 12–16
feminist critics, 4, 12–14
feminist film historiography, 107–9
Ferrante, Elena, 18, 41
Five Easy Pieces, 77
flops. *See* box-office flops/ bombs
freedom, 75

gangster film(s), 137, 143; *Mikey and
Nikey* as, 5, 71, 137. *See also* mob
"gangster girl," May as, 84, 131
gender. *See* female directors; masculinity
Genette, Gérard, 73–74

genre(s), 6, 114; May and, 4, 6, 7, 13, 113,
114. *See also specific genres*
Ghostbusters II, 35, 124n33
ghostwriting, 36, 139
gimmicks, 51; Hollywood, 51, 99–103
Ginsburg, Ruth Bader, 9–10, 120
Good Fight, The, 9–10, 120
Grace, Carol, 68, 79, 85
Graduate, The, 111; *Enter Laughing* and,
38, *38*; *The Heartbreak Kid* and, 55, 56,
66, 67, 125n43
"Green Heart, A" (Ritchie), 43, 52, 65
Grodin, Charles: in *The Heartbreak Kid*,
23, 57–58, 60, 125n43, 134; *Ishtar* and,
106, 112
Guest, Haden, 13; on Cassavetes, 132–34;
on Falk, 132, 146; interactions with
May, 84; on May, 42; on May's films, 6,
108; May's interviews with, 112, 129–47

Hankin, Annette, 19–20, 80
Harnick, Sheldon, 17
Harris, Barbara, 21
Harris, Mark, 18–20, 22
Haskell, Molly, 4, 7, 11, 71–72, 126n52;
on May, 123n14; *Mikey and Nicky* and,
71–72, 123n14; on portrayal of women
in May's films, 14
Heartbreak Kid, The, 24, 43–45, 62–67,
63, 125nn46–47; assimilation and
distance, 53–61; camerawork, 53–58,
70; characterizations of, 30, 44–45, 66,
67; Charles Grodin in, 23, 57–58, 60,
125n43, 134; compared with *A New
Leaf,* 5, 7, 14, 15, 20, 21, 26, 30–32,
40–45, 47–48, 52, 58–59, 66–67; Ethan
Warren on, 56–57, 64–66; gender roles
in, 7, 14, 21; *The Graduate* and, 55, 56,
66, 67, 125n43; improvisation in, 23–24,
124n26; Jeannie Berlin in, 45, 131 (*see
also* Lila Kolodny); Joe McElhaney on,
40, 57, 61, 65, 125n47; May on, 136;
May's direction in, 23, 47–48, 56–57, 61,
64; Neil Simon and, 23, 32, 53–55, 57,
64, 65; plot, 41; script/screenplay, 23,
48, 53–55, 64, 65; temporal compres-
sion/rushing in, 40–41; as an unromantic
comedy, 41–43. *See also* Lenny Cantrow

Johnson, Dakota, 37
jokes, 30, 31, 138–39; ethnic, 33, 100–101; in *Ishtar*, 93, 97, 100–101, 104; May's, 10, 33–34, 45, 46, 48 (see also under *Ishtar*); May's reactions to, 25; sexist, 100–101; visual, 45. *See also* humor journalists. *See* media

Kael, Pauline, 27, 45, 64, 65
Kafka, Franz, 33
Kahn, Sheldon, 83
klutziness, 21

Lane, Christina, 117
Last Detail, The, 77
Lenny Cantrow (character in *The Heartbreak Kid*), 30, 32, 62; alone and adrift, 66, *66*; assimilation and distance, 53–61, *56*; as ethnic interloper, 32, 61, *61*; Jewishness, 32, 53, 61; keeping him at a distance, 55, *56*; relationship with Lila Kolodny (wife), 21, 41, 42, 48, 53–57, 62, 65, 66
Lila Kolodny (character in *The Heartbreak Kid*), 20, 43, 58; Jeannie Berlin as, 40, 45, 55, 65, 131; Jewishness, 65, 125n47; May on, 55; as negatively-portrayed character, 54–55; placing the audience on Lila's "side," 57, 58; relationship with Lenny Cantrow (husband), 21, 41, 42, 48, 53–57, 62, 65, 66
Loden, Barbara, 79–80
Lonergan, Kenneth, 40–41. See also *Waverly Gallery*
Luv, 35, 37–39

machismo, 8, 70
mafia, 141. *See also* mob
male idiocy, 5, 43, 93
mannerisms, 21
Martha, 125n46
Martin, Steve, 127n72
Marty Freed (character in *Ishtar*), 89, 99–100, 107; "sing songs people know," 100, *100*
masculinity, 8, 14, 15, 61; compulsive masculinity and 1970s cinema, 75–81;

directors and, 114; *Ishtar* and, 89, 91, 93, 94; *Mikey and Nicky* and, 67–70, 75–76, 131. *See also* male idiocy
Matthau, Walter, 24, 43
May, Elaine: acting of (*see* acting); awards and honors, 11, 22, 36, 119; "born in a trunk," 16–17; characterizations of, 4, 6, 9–11, 18–20, 27–28, 69, 84, 124n28, 131; early life, 16–18; family background, 16; finances, 9, 43–44, 106, 109, 133; interviews of (*see* interviews of May); marriages, 17; men explain things to, 20–22; men she dated, 19, 20; people's efforts to "reshape" or "improve," 20–21; personality, 13, 18–20, 26, 28, 109–10 (*see also* perfectionism); photographic memory, 83; privacy, 4, 18; pseudonyms, 27, 35; public appearances, 18; publications about, 11; residence, 17; reticence, 18 (*see also* reticent approach); signature verbal tendencies, 33–34; silence, 4, 18; training, 24, 25. *See also specific topics*
"May Renaissance," 11, 122n10
McElhaney, Joseph "Joe," 6, 57, 69–70, 78, 79, 125n44, 127n67; on *The Heartbreak Kid*, 40, 57, 61, 65, 125n47
media, 17, 115, 117; May in the, 4, 9, 20, 21; May's aversion to the, 4, 17
Meisner, Sanford "Sandy," 87–88, 135
Method acting, 69
Middle East, 89, 92, 101–2. See also *Ishtar*
Mike Nichols: American Masters (documentary), 22, 118–19, 121
Mikey and Nicky: an unforgiving light, 76, *76*; auteurism and, 11, 69, 70; camerawork, 68–70, 78–79; Cassavetes in, 24, 25, 67–68, 70, 82–85, 87, 88, 132, 144–46; characterizations of, 70, 125n48 (*see also* gangster film[s]: *Mikey and Nikey* as); cliché and, 73–75; digression and masculine dysfunction, 67–71 (*see also* under masculinity); improvisation and, 24, 82; Julian Schlossberg on, 82, 126n54; May on, 73; May's direction in, 24–25, 78, 82;

Warren, Ethan, 56–57, 64–66
Wasson, Sam, 97, 124n33
"Water Cooler" (skit), 39, 121
Waverly Gallery, The, 9, 40–41, 119
Way of All Fish, The (play), 32–33
Weill, Claudia, 8, 108–10, 116
Williams, Paul, 106
Wilson, Edmund, 19, 28, 124n37
Wolf, 22, 35–37, 102
women. *See* female directors; misogyny; sexism

writer, May as, 19, 36; characterizations of, 37; pseudonyms, 27, 35; style, 3. *See also* ghostwriting; plays of May; screenplays of May; scripts
writerly style of May, 81–88

Yablans, Frank "Frankie," 87, 126n62, 132, 136, 137
Yiddishism, 51

Elizabeth Alsop is an assistant professor of communication and media at the CUNY School of Professional Studies and a faculty member in Film and Media Cultures at the CUNY Graduate Center. She is the author of *Making Conversation in Modernist Fiction*.

The University of Illinois Press
is a founding member of the
Association of University Presses.

———————————————

Composed in 10/13 New Caledonia
with Helvetica Neue display
by Lisa Connery
at the University of Illinois Press
Manufactured by Sheridan Books, Inc.

University of Illinois Press
1325 South Oak Street
Champaign, IL 61820–6903
www.press.uillinois.edu